Yours, Mine, and Ours

Yours, Mine, and Ours

Creating a Compelling Donor Experience

BARRY J. MCLEISH

BICENTENNIAL
1807
WILEY
2007
BICENTENNIAL

John Wiley & Sons, Inc.

For general information on our other products and services, or technical support, please contact our Customer Care Department within the United States at 800-762-2974, outside the United States at 317-572-3993 or fax 317-572-4002.

Wiley also publishes its books in a variety of electronic formats. Some content that appears in print may not be available in electronic books.

For more information about Wiley products, visit our Web site at http://www.wiley.com.

Library of Congress Cataloging-in-Publication Data:

ISBN: 978-0-470-12640-0

Printed in the United States of America

10 9 8 7 6 5 4 3 2 1

For James, David, Pete, Ron, Larry, and Mark

Contents

Preface

Great achievements in the nonprofit world often occur when institutions harness their own internal energy and simultaneously, that of individuals around them and deal purposefully with an aspect of our nation or of any nation that needs intervention. Collectively they create for the briefest of moments a joint and reciprocally driven, caring, trusting, community. Being accountable for the common good and the welfare of those needing help is assumed by all parties in the community and is a part of their underlying ideals and beliefs.

This has been my personal experience as a donor to a variety of causes. The urgency and ego of "me" is subsumed in the "we," as, bundled together with other donors and volunteers, I have contributed to solving an impending or immediate social problem, or have helped take advantage of a new opportunity that benefits a group of individuals in need. Thousands of men and women around the world had similar experiences during the New York terrorist crisis of September 2001, and again after the Asian tsunami, the Kashmir earthquake, and the New Orleans flooding disaster, as they took part in a worldwide collective show of support for those who had fallen.

However, what of those times in everyday life when there is not an all-consuming societal crisis to draw everyone together? Some nonprofit executives feel the notion of civic sharing and involvement is in danger of being stripped away from society as it becomes seemingly harder to convince some individuals of its worth. These same institutional executives wonder whether many of our nation's potential donors and volunteers are simply too narrowly self-serving in their approach to life. Is it possible, they ask, that the notion of civic joining is being eclipsed by a society that seems with every passing day to have room only for a collective "I" at its center? A society whose very notions of success seem at odds with caring for those who cannot succeed at the same level?

Do the questions our society currently seems preoccupied with—"What do I need today?" "What must I do to succeed?" and "Where will I find fulfillment?"—increasingly preclude civic and moral involvement? What effect do such issues as environmental and moral concerns, the nation's economic outlook and the ripple effect it has had on investors and foundation giving, not to mention unemployment, have on stakeholder involvement?

There is some justification for these expressed concerns. Although average household income is approximately $42,000 per year and philanthropic giving is increasing across the United States (representing an $800 billion industry employing nearly 11 million people and contributing 10% to our nation's economy), it still represents just slightly more than 2% of the nation's gross domestic product. Some higher-earning income groups give at less than half this, and many wealthy individuals are no longer able to give at the rates they gave during boom times.[1]

Perhaps not surprisingly, some statistics show many wealthy taxpayers have actually retreated from charitable giving.[2] In contrast, some lower-income brackets now contribute a higher percentage of their earnings to charities than individuals in other brackets. There seems to still be money available for individuals to give. Just a few years ago, *Fast Company* columnist Tony Schwartz quoted the Newtithing Group, a San Francisco–based nonprofit organization that promotes philanthropy, as suggesting that Americans could have given an additional $250 billion to charity without decreasing their net worth.[3] In an interview with Stan Guthrie, professor of public policy and theology at Eastern Baptist

Theological Seminary, author Ron Sider suggested in *Christianity Today* that if the average Christian were to tithe, an additional $143 billion dollars would be given to philanthropic causes.[4]

However, a number of Americans choose not to follow suit. Why? Although there could be many reasons for this apparent lack of action, a key one may lie within the nonprofit agencies themselves. Regardless of how well those in need may be served, many organizations have done a poor job of engaging donors', customers', and volunteers' feelings and emotions in a satisfactory way—what Rolf Jensen, the director of the Copenhagen Institute for Future Studies, calls, "emotional jogging."[5] As a result of this lack of satisfactory engagement, some third-sector observers have joined political scientist Everett Carll Ladd in asking, "Aren't we retreating into private pursuits, or to use a metaphor that has resonated in recent years, aren't we increasingly 'bowling alone?'"[6]

Though some of the concerns nonprofit directors cite regarding the lack of donor and volunteer involvement within their own organizations might seem plausible in our competitive fundraising climate today, aspects of their argument also miss the mark. It may be true that for a select group of individuals, their current involvement with causes they support is churning heavily and in flux; it is equally true that many of these same causes are changing their methods of operation to allow donors and volunteers access to their organizational mix and inner workings in a way previously not thought of as possible or even appropriate.[7] Additionally, other organizations are pooling their efforts with agencies in similar categories of service, consolidating work loads, reducing costs of operation, and in the process, creating a new critical mass of service.

Philanthropic tastes are also changing and contributing to this churn, especially given the large number of individuals who no longer feel content to simply give financial gifts to charities.[8] For many donors, being philanthropic now means not only choosing where their financial gift will go but showing active interest, concern, and involvement with the recipient organization, with subsequent follow-up on how their gift is used.

The telemarketing team for a client noted that in a recent campaign, among those who responded affirmatively to their fund-raising calls, two different response segments emerged. The first segment consisted of those who asked no questions when engaged by the solicitor and got off the phone as quickly as possible after responding affirmatively or negatively. The second segment responded to the offer with a qualified "yes," only after asking a series of questions about the cause's request and engaging the operator in conversation about detailed aspects of the program.*

*From the personal client files of Barry McLeish.

When added up, instances like this may not point to a widespread decline in societal involvement with the philanthropic world. Rather, the opposite might be true. A dramatic change in philanthropic involvement could be taking place within some sectors of the population in the light of individual initiatives and personal preferences. For these sectors of society, a massive social and cultural revolution is at work, particularly in the way individuals relate to nonprofit organizations and each other, affecting what they will and will not support and what they expect from such philanthropic involvement.

These societal changes are as real as the moral mandate most nonprofit organizations have in bringing help and providing hope to those in trouble and in need. They represent the "new normal" that institutions will have to contend with.[9] *Yours, Mine, and Ours: Creating a Compelling Donor Experience* is a book about enabling this type of change to take place at an even deeper level organizationally by giving those who donate money and/or their time, or purchase nonprofit products, a compelling and rewarding experience and a reason to continue to involve themselves within the organization's philanthropic world.

■ NOTES

1. Kirsner, Scott, "Nonprofit Motive," Wired, September, 1999, p. 110. Guthrie, Stan, "The Evangelical Scandal," Christianity Today, April 2005, p. 71.

2. Rosenberg, Claude Jr., Wealthy and Wise (New York: Little, Brown & Company, 1994), p. 15.

3. Schwartz, Tony, "Tell the Truth," Fast Company, August 2000, p. 228.

4. Guthrie, Stan, "The Evangelical Scandal," Christianity Today, April 2005, p. 71.

5. Jensen, Rolf, The Dream Society: How the Coming Shift from Information to Imagination Will Transform Your Business (New York: McGraw-Hill, 1999).

6. Ladd, Everett Carll, The Ladd Report (New York: The Free Press, 1999), p. 2.

7. Oates, Mary J., "How the Catholic Church Made Giving Decline," The Chronicle of Philanthropy, March 21, 1996, p. 50.

8. Mitchell, Emily, "Getting Better at Doing Good," Time, February 21, 2000, p. B9.

9. McNamee, Roger, as quoted by Polly LaBarre, Fast Company, May 2003, p. 78.

Introduction

I n 1964, within the pages of the *Harvard Business Review*, Warren Bennis and Philip Slater wrote that democracy was a system of values superior to all others. The shared and collaborative values democracy mirrored—and the authors wrote of—were more than a collection of good ideas, maxims, motives, and attitudes. In fact, according to both authors, these values were vital to the process of any group trying to reach goals in a systematic way.

Although our world has been remade many times over since the article was written, similar observations can be made about many nonprofit agencies today. Democratic values are at work in this marketplace in a new way. Many organizations are evidencing a type of democratic community in their workplace that is part of a much larger societal transformation, one that demands new realities, trust, structures, and competitive strategies from the institutions caught up in it.

This pervasive transformation is everywhere and is unavoidably encountered in the day-to-day workings of almost all nonprofit organizations. In fact, many nonprofit managerial and marketing consultants and theorists routinely suggest that institutional and managerial change is the "next big thing," an unavoidable phenomenon in the nonprofit world as a result of this transformation. As our country looks backward at the rise of global capitalism and the demise of communism along with the failures of so many social programs to create wealth and equality, and forward to the largest generational shift in our country's history, the pundits are stating the obvious: Environmental and economic change is, in fact, the most perplexing issue many nonprofit institutions face now or will ever face.

However, behind concerns for the future is a more immediate question many organizations address with varying degrees of success: "What will our organization do about the changes upon us right now?"

Notions of change are common to those who work in the nonprofit world, as is the pressures to change. What *feels* new, however, is the ever-increasing sense some nonprofit organization leaders have that they *must* change; that maintaining the status quo is not only ill-advised but harmful and, in some cases, destructive to their institutions. This sentiment is continuously reinforced by the for-profit business press, seminars, and many consultants, who imply that organizations must be constantly going through some sort of introspective, serious, and ongoing managerial and opera-tional transformation to be properly managed.

Nonprofit institutional leaders are not immune to these prag-matic, psychological pressures. The reasons for this are quite simple. In many nonprofit institutions there is no longer a quality gap between the services they provide and those being provided by similar groups with like-minded societal visions and causal offerings. Not only are there multiple nonprofit organizations providing the same or similar services, but donors, customers, and volunteers can typically find significant cross-sector overlap with the services being provided by for-profit and governmental institutions, as in the following example.

REAL-WORLD EXAMPLES

A close friend who uses a wheelchair has the option of taking a specially designed city bus to get around (paid for by taxes), taking a special van (funded by a grant-giving institution) run

by an assisted-living organization, or riding in a special church
van (paid for by parishioner donations). These rides have no
financial charge directed at the rider; all have to be scheduled,
all are relatively safe, and all deliver my friend to where he
wants to go.

These marketplace conditions have contributed to creating more
discerning donors and customers who possess a higher expectation
of what to look for—and demand from—nonprofit customer
services. What is called "shareholder value" or "brand equity value"
in the for-profit world—the dominant driving force in business for
the past few years—is also being felt and expressed in the nonprofit
world. Here it takes the form of consumer and donor expectations
of better stakeholder experiences, service, timeliness of response,
vision, and performance on the part of institutions they support and
are interested in. The need to create a compelling philanthropic
experience and bond—whether for a donor, a volunteer, a board
member, or a customer—is the benchmark that most organizations
must set their sights on and operate against.

Because of these pressures, it is also a confusing time for some
nonprofit executives and directors. On the one hand, donors, board
members, and other key stakeholders hold leaders accountable for
making the changes that will better serve the organizations they
are involved with. On the other hand, individuals in the same
stakeholder groups sometimes suggest that nonprofit agency change
is not occurring rapidly enough. Some go so far as to state that many
of the intractable social ills society faces have become this way as a
result of a retreat from social realities on the part of managers and
their often half-baked responses to the challenges these social needs
represent. As was suggested previously, some nonprofit organizations unfortunately aren't dealing with these societal and environmental phenomena, while others are simply responding in the

wrong way. Still other institutional leaders, often feeling uncertainty and fear, are choosing to do nothing.

Because society and the structures within it—including the nonprofit landscape—are changing quickly and expansively, it is difficult for any one organization or individual leader to follow all the developments. Therefore, it is easy to see why some institutional leaders react fearfully or stumble as they try to create strategies quickly enough to confront their competitive environments.

With the economic landscape and operating structure of so many nonprofit industries changing, so must the nature of their work and the way they define success. Unfortunately, some organizations deny the possible institutional impact of these environmental and competitive changes and simply choose to ignore signals that could tell them what is happening to their customers, volunteers, and donors. Surprisingly, this not an unusual response. Research prior to September 11, 2001 suggested that more than 95% of the for-profit executives polled felt their organizations could handle any economic turbulence they might face (Colvin,1999). Given the pragmatic and psychological proximity of the nonprofit and for-profit fields, there is reason to believe some nonprofit executives would have said the same thing if asked.

However, not all nonprofit organizational executives feel this way. "The changes coming in the next five years can easily be seen as both threatening and fearful," warns Lisa Olsen, a nonprofit marketing consultant in the Midwest. "Everyone is being impacted but not everyone understands what to do."[1]

To be sure, none of us can see the future clearly. What nonprofit executives can do is to prepare themselves for different environmental and organizational possibilities in the days ahead in which new levels of competition will constantly breach old rules of operating. When Jerry Porras and Jim Collins wrote *Built to Last* (1994), they suggested companies had to learn the paradoxical notions of continuity and change in their management and leadership. Within the current turbulent and polarized landscape, some nonprofit organizations find themselves dealing with what is often perceived as "new" or "extravagant" stakeholder demands from individuals who feel they have not only a large stake in the organizations they support but a right to have a say in organizational affairs, issues of mission, managerial continuity, and change. These developments are at the forefront of many nonprofit leadership discussions. In fact, countless organizations that want to succeed will have to create new forms of stakeholder value in ways that are different and perhaps strange to their corporate cultures.

However, organizations spending the time, effort, and necessary resources to build trust networks to meet new stakeholder demands are also learning to create value for all within their institutions. As a result of this process, new causal endeavors are entering the U.S. philanthropic marketplace in record numbers and new types of collaborative partnerships and equity are coming to those involved. These intangible assets are also playing an increasing "non-book" role in creating value for nonprofit organizations.

In short, many organizations are creating a compelling experience for the donors, customers, and volunteers involved with them by encouraging the creation of lifestyle associations and social networks of like-minded individuals, based on their perceptions of what is right and necessary both for the public and for the nonprofit organization they are involved with.

Some authors, consultants, and practitioners are labeling this effort—and the organizational culture required—the "new philanthropy," signifying a truly different period in philanthropic history.[2] For the organizations this applies to, this period is also marked by mutual risk on the part of both donor and organization, with performance benchmarks and expectations being suggested overtly by all parties and worked out jointly between them. Modeled on the notion of "strategic partners" in the commercial world, donors, volunteers, and customers build trust relationships with the organizations they support. Instead of the organization solely controlling the communication and relationship, risk is shared by both parties as is a heightened concern for the end goals of the organization. Although "risk" has always been integral to the philanthropic process, what is different is the open acknowledgment of it by all parties. Consequently, a new breed of "social entrepreneur," "venture donor," and "radical philanthropist" is emerging, along with hundreds of new charities, some Internet based.

Currently, more money is being given to nonprofit organizations than ever before. Increases in the new millennium are coming on the heels of increases during previous years, with charitable donations increasing by half from 1990 to 2001. In addition, what typically dominates the discussions regarding the "new philanthropy" is the attitude and the outside-the-box approach some outspoken philanthropists are taking.

Often relatively "young" in their relationship to the philanthropic industry and their new-found wealth, these individuals are accustomed to making things happen quickly in their own corporate and professional worlds. Further, they have strong feelings about how the nonprofit institutions they are interested in should be run, managed, and funded, as well as the tasks they should be involved in.

As has been widely covered by the business and national press, social entrepreneurs have sought to herald a new day in how society helps those in need through a reinvention of generosity. The often-cited philanthropic model of an older woman sitting alone at home, writing a check to an agency as a result of a direct mail appeal, with virtually no reciprocal involvement with the organization is unappealing to these mavericks. For some philanthropic entrepreneurs, a compelling nonprofit experience has resulted in the creation of online giving malls, which donate a portion of their profits to charities. Others have advocated the use of the Internet's mind-numbing capabilities in being able to supply prodigious amounts of information that can be used as one-stop philanthropy guides, allowing an individual to research a charity, request specific information, print out donation forms, and donate money using a credit card. Still others are creating new models of charities involving the mentoring, training, and empowering of community leaders.

Although the outcomes of some of these new initiatives remain to be seen, what is observable is that many social entrepreneurs have managed to advance to doing something in their own way as a "right" they see themselves entitled to, creating new models of philanthropic involvement that have become a benchmark and organizational structure in and of themselves. Hundreds of philanthropic projects are being driven today by the interests, passions, and abilities of social entrepreneurs young and old, all having the firm belief that their way is better than the methodologies organizations they are interested in currently employ. For example, according to Stacy Palmer, editor of *The Chronicle of Philanthropy*, in medical research, "business-world donors have gotten fed up with the slow, tradition-bound world of medical research, where scientific breakthroughs can take decades to become treatments that people can use. These givers expect concrete results for their cash. They demand a return on their investment."[3]

Working with donors who wish to *go their own way* has proven difficult for some institutions, particularly many mainline agencies used to *telling* donors how they should handle their philanthropic pursuits. Coming from a tradition where leaders make decisions and subordinates carry them out, classical management theory has not always been helpful to nonprofit leaders and managers in confronting these new situations. No longer able to rely on loyalty as a marketplace imperative, these institutions must often contend with venture philanthropists who desire to create hybrid programs or seriously want to refocus existing organizational efforts in personal ways. Simply giving away their money is too passive for these individuals. Many want to be involved in ambitious projects that demand results and have mutually attached strings between organization and donor. "Rather than just writing hefty annual checks to old-line charities, they are bringing their problem-solving skills and natural-born impatience to the fight."[4] However, the notion of allowing a "donor-designated project or fund"—created by a donor because he or she believes it is right as opposed to funding a project created by the organization—is simply unacceptable to some nonprofit leaders who may view these upstart philanthropists as disloyal individualists.

In much the same vein, a variety of journals and articles have suggested this new generation of potential and actual donors are skeptical of the "business and performance" of philanthropies and desire to maintain full control over their giving and the disbursement of gifts whenever and however they want. This clashing of cultures and styles has led some to controversy in the philanthropic field.[5]

Some of today's donors simply do not understand why nonprofit organizations work as they do, often apparently willing to gloss over and prolong programmatic failures. On the other hand, many institutions wonder whether entrepreneurial philanthropists will ever understand how difficult it is to undertake some of the humanitarian efforts nonprofit institutions initiate and are a part of. Consequently, philanthropy is going through great flux and uncertainty. For some to organizational leaders, donors, and authors caught up in these discussions, trust in each other is at a premium.

Correspondingly, there is now a systemic change taking place in the hearts and minds of a number of philanthropists and nonprofit leaders across this country in how they deal with each other. This change, when taken seriously by the two parties, often requires an attitudinal and operational transformation on the part of both individuals and institutions. Unfortunately, nonprofit managers not involved in this ongoing process of organizational and stakeholder redefinition face an exceedingly difficult and competitive future with both current and emergent donor pools. Additionally, the stakes are high in this redefinition process because of the presence of new wealth, as well as the much-heralded transference of wealth in the years ahead. Some consultants and authors suggest anywhere from $6 trillion to $20 trillion could be transferred to charities through wills and gifts over the next 50 years.

To take advantage of this income transference will require new models of nonprofit leadership and stakeholder participation. Unfortunately, in disaggregating some of today's nonprofit organizations into their respective components, one often finds little more than lip service paid to the importance of popular managerial imperatives of the past few years (e.g., stakeholder values, the importance of each person's contribution within an organization, etc.). Further, on peeling back bureaucratic layers, the same observer may find vestiges of old-style command-and-control governance methods being used to cover poor leadership practices, as well as hierarchical layers of management that do not contribute to the successful day-to-day tactics of the organization or create value for employees, donors, or other stakeholders. Unless corrected, these relatively common nonprofit organizational pathologies can lead institutions to a downward spiral of poor performance and organizational self-destruction. As a consequence, little room is left for the many operational concerns and questions donors and volunteers may have.

While it is often true that there are few natural, internal constituencies demanding change from within many nonprofit organizations, it is increasingly clear that some institutions require new operational models that are sensitive to donor concerns and market-savvy customers, as well as to the environmental context within which they operate. For many of these agencies, there is an additional need to address the churning, destabilizing effects innovative nonprofit organizations are having upon some previously stable causal markets. In dozens of markets and concerns, from youth camps to foreign mission boards, to civic institutions caring for the poor and indigent, new organizational models are emerging. Consequently, organizational agility must become part of an institution's DNA as managers seek to change, adapt, and shed old models that no longer apply. With intense global concerns and competition facing some nonprofit organizations, along with their need for alignment between various supporting groups and intra-organizational relationships, a new spirit of collaboration, democracy, and values orientation is being forced on various institutions. In addition, diversity and consensus-building issues are contributing to the need for new methods of operation.

Author and statesman Vaclav Havel noted a number of years ago, "Something is on the way out, and something else is painfully being born."[6] Can the majority of nonprofit leaders face and accommodate the painful realities being born in today's marketplace, realities requiring them to become skilled in negotiation, integration, persuasion, and listening? Can these same men and women manage the new values of empowerment and trust alive in their patrons, as well as the unique viewpoints some of their constituents hold, while also satisfying the needs of those who have lent their organizations' allegiance over the years through volunteerism, donations, and other types of support? With these "centrifugal forces of diversity and interdependence" at work in the life of institutions, how will nonprofit leaders and their associates survive in the days ahead?"[7]

The reality is that many nonprofit organizations will have a hard time surviving, especially given the difficulty some are already experiencing with marketplace changes they currently face. Though Washington officials in the Clinton era suggested America was in the throes of a "charity boom," philanthropy still amounted to approximately 2% of the gross domestic product, and personal giving represented 1.8% of personal income, a number that could easily be larger without affecting personal wealth accumulation for most individuals.[8] Some characterize today's culture as increasingly, "Wall Street–like, one that celebrates the twin propositions that 'greed is good' and 'more is better.'"[9] Authors, such as Paulina

Borsook in her book *Cyberselfish*, wonder whether many business leaders will be philanthropic in any meaningful way.

In this environment, many nonprofit leaders routinely work with the marketing *rules* and funding formulas they have been taught at dozens of seminars during the past several years, only to find many of them simply no longer work in the situations these leaders find themselves in. What should they be doing that they currently aren't? What do donors and other constituents really want? Answers to these questions as well as many other pertinent marketing issues are within reach in the pages of *Yours, Mine, and Ours: Creating a Compelling Donor Experience*.

ORGANIZATION OF THIS BOOK

These are extremely interesting and in some cases difficult times for nonprofit leaders and managers. What type of philanthropic society are they inheriting? How will they strategically navigate their organizations in the light of institutional productivity and great marketplace uncertainty? In Chapter 1, today's for-profit and nonprofit managerial and organizational environment is described, including the way both society and many business models are being upended, often by Internet and new e-commerce models. Looking at issues of increased stakeholder expectations in the light of the rising consumer power of donors, customers, and volunteers, the increasing strain this is having upon all levels of nonprofit leadership is documented. Setting the stage for the rest of the book, Chapter 1 also looks at issues of managerial and institutional culture in light of a marketplace where knowing how to ask the right questions is now often more profitable than pretending to have the right answer.

When an organization is tossed to and fro managerially or is facing critical tactical decisions, the best plan in turbulent times is to have a clear strategy. How do nonprofit organizations develop a *clear strategy* in the light of environmental uncertainty? Chapter 2 suggests that the first part of this answer is found by more closely following donors, volunteers, and customers to see where they are going, discovering the values they exhibit and hold close, and then working to integrate these expectations within the organization's. The net effect of balancing these two often seemingly contradictory groups is to create organizations that have the capacity to truly serve society, supportive stakeholders, and organizational members simultaneously.

Chapter 3 gives another part of the answer to this complicated issue of strategy by looking at how institutions can begin the process of transforming themselves in a manner that is purposely tied to their organizational competencies, leadership capabilities, and the expectations of their stakeholders. Many institutions—for-profit and nonprofit—have a hard time renewing themselves. Those traditionally bounded sometimes feel change undermines their revered histories. John Gardner, the founder of Common Cause and later cofounder of the Independent Sector, notes, "the more high minded an institution, the harder it is to renew. Those of you who have been in this field know that it is very easy for a nonprofit institution to become a legend in its own mind."[10] Unfortunately, it is becoming increasingly useless to discuss institutions that do not transform themselves; nonprofit directors have inherited a world where constant human renewal and organizational transformation are expected mandates of donative and other supportive communities.

Chapters 4 and 5 suggest that what is needed for many organizations is a different strategic path nonprofit organizational leadership can follow, a path governed by a series of new operational rules or guidelines institutions can navigate by that are grounded in documented evidence and benchmarked as best practices by nonprofit and sometimes for-profit organizations. Rather than repackage old approaches and then put a new face on them—often suggested by directors who would rather operate safely than propose solutions requiring organizational and personal change—what is suggested in these chapters are new steps others have taken and found helpful. Bill Shore, executive director of the nonprofit organization Share Our Strength notes in *Revolution of the Heart*, "It's as if we drive around the block, over and over, always surprised and disappointed that we end up in the same place. And while we've spent more and more money to make the trip in bigger cars with better engines, we only get to the same place faster each time, but do not get anywhere new."[11] Chapters 4 and 5 specify the new directions nonprofit organizations need to travel in order to survive and excel in today's marketplace.

Building on themes from Chapters 4 and 5, Chapter 6 calls on nonprofit organizations to no longer rely on how they operated yesterday to justify what they are doing today. The chapter suggests that nothing stops organizations from succeeding more quickly than continuing to operate as if nothing ever changed. What is sufficient for today will not necessarily work tomorrow. Reflecting a heartfelt impatience with the status quo, a new operational mentality must become the guiding principle for all nonprofit organizations, whether they are looking at the rules their organizational culture dictates, their marketing and management systems, or the causal programs they run.

This attitude raises a question: "How then does an organization build a strategically sound infrastructure and capacity that survives the churn of today and tomorrow and serves stakeholders? Continuing a theme started in Chapter 6 and running through Chapter 8, five foundational answers to this question are explained in detail.

■ **NOTES**

1. *Personal conversation with author at the Tinning Symposium, April 17, 2000, in San Antonio, Texas.*
2. *Byrne, John A., "The New Face of Philanthropy,"* Businessweek, *December 2, 2002, pp. 82–94.*

3. Daniels, Cora, "The Man Who Changed Medicine, Fortune, *November 29, 2004, p. 94.*

4. *Ibid., p. 94.*

5. *Frumkin, Peter, "A New Era in Giving,"* The Washington Post National Weekly Edition, *October 11, 1999, p. 22.*

6. *Havel, Vaclav, "The New Measure of Man,"* New York Times, *July 8, 1994, Op-Ed page.*

7. *Lipman-Blumen, Jean, "Connective Leadership: A New Paradigm," in* Drucker Management, *Spring 1997, p. 15.*

8. *Allen, Kent, "Not Giving 'Til It Hurts,'"* The Washington Post National Weekly Edition, *June 5, 2000, p. 34.*

9. *Collins, Jim, "Built to Flip,"* Fast Company, *March, 2000, p. 132.*

10. *Gardner, John, "Renewal of Philanthropy and the Independent Sector," in* Giving Back to the Future: Philanthropy in the Twenty-First Century, *Community Foundations of the San Francisco Bay Area, September 28, 1998, p. 41.*

11. *Shore, Bill,* Revolution of the Heart *(New York: Riverhead Books, 1995), p. 15.*

■ REFERENCES

Borsook, Paulina, *Cyberselfish* (New York: Public Affairs, 2000).

Collins, James C. and Jerry I. Porras, *Built to Last* (New York: Harper-Business, 1994).

Colvin, Geoffrey, "When It Comes to Turbulence, CEO's Could Learn a Lot from Sailors," *Fortune*, March 29, 1999.

Slater, Philip and Warren G. Bennis, "Democracy Is Inevitable," *Harvard Business Review,* March–April, 1964.

Acknowledgments

H ope is not lost for those at work in the philanthropic world. There is good news to report. Literally hundreds of nonprofit organizations are not only weathering the societal, funding, and cultural storms they are facing today, but are prospering in spite of them. Some are prospering because of them.

My associates at McConkey/Johnston can testify to this. Across the United States, Canada, Mexico, and Great Britain, we see thousands of men and women working side by side with institutions of change and benevolence in highly purposeful ways, in both civic and religious communities. They are heroes to us. To them and to the associates I work with, I owe a debt of appreciation, especially in their helping to inspire some of the remarks in this book. Bill McConkey, Larry Johnston, Jeff McLinden, Jan Urbec, Bruce Cole, Sally Funk, Ron Frey, Redina Kolaneci, and Margaret Winn, my colleagues at McConkey-Johnston have contributed without knowing as I learned from working with them.

Pete Sommer, Larry Fuhrer, Ron Ward, and Lisa Olsen helped considerably in the early formation of this text, as did Bill Chickering, Cindy Miglietti, Carolyn Hansen-Arnold, Bernice Ledbetter, Ralph Stewart, Cathi Woods, and, finally, Judy Packard and Mark Olson before their untimely deaths. Shelly Mutch, Don Mercer, and Brian Ogne brought unique nonprofit marketing perspectives to bear, and John and Kathy Fitts-Porter helped articulate corporate and for-profit marketing realities. Kim Evans and Keith McNair forced the text to be relevant to Canadian and

European standards, and Bob Silverman of the Fielding Institute helped define the importance of this inquiry.

John Wiley & Sons, Inc., Senior Editor Susan M. McDermott and Senior Production Editor Natasha Wolfe were of great help with their wise comments, commitment and enthusiastic support.

Close friends Roberta, James, Robin, Barbara, and David read early portions of the manuscript and suggested how to make it better.

Finally, Deborah Lynn Porter McLeish provided quiet miracles in spite of her busy medical practice.

There is a Scottish proverb that says, "Where the heart's past hope, the face is past shame."

I am not past hope. Nor are these colleagues and associates I have named. We live in a world where only a small percentage of the population has the ability and resources to buy and read this book. We are blessed and privileged to be where we are today. Therefore, I join you, the reader, in never being at a place emotionally where we are beyond shame and hope in our daily pursuit of changing this world as we know it for the better.

CHAPTER 1

Redefining Boundaries

The nonprofit sector has within it the ability to create a combined virtue that goes far beyond anything the government or the for-profit sector provides. Michael O'Neill, the director of the Institute for Nonprofit Organization Management, suggests, "the independent sector can experiment with new strategies of social action, respond quickly to new social needs, and generally provide 'social risk capital.' "[1] However, the nonprofit sector has never been tested as it is being now. The challenges to it are stunning both in their breadth and their complexity. At a time when the United States seems no longer confidently progressive in many areas of social engagement nor certain of its moral center, and with internal and external tensions threatening both the central wellbeing of the country as well as its relationships with the rest of the world, how should nonprofit sector organizations navigate? How should they go about creating a compelling donor or volunteer experience for the stakeholders entrusted to their care?

These questions have never been more important than right now, simply because so many in our society—those in need of the services nonprofit organizations provide, those providing the services, taxpayers, elected officials, donors, volunteers, and communities at large—have a stake in seeing strong improvements within the public or third sector of this country. Many of the protections once in place to help those in need of these services are being dismantled by cities, states, and our nation's government in disagreements over financial priorities, or are being curtailed by inflationary or political pressures. Nonprofit organizations no longer have a straight path to run on. They are often in flux, requiring constant managerial flexibility and marketing reorientation.

AMERICAN PHILANTHROPY

There is unprecedented need in the United States today. There is also unprecedented affluence. America emerged from the trauma of World War II as the richest, most powerful nation in the world, having been neither invaded nor financially ravaged. Today, mass affluence is a societal reality, accessible to many. Even families living at the poverty level in America live better than 75% of the world. In fact, the wealthy in the United States reputedly have so much money, it is frequently cited by seminar and nonprofit leaders that if they pooled their resources together, America's affluent could feed the world's poor and still live comfortably. Whether this is true or not is open to debate, but what is true is that American benevolence is stronger than that of virtually any other country in the world, and the United States is the most generous nation in regard to contributed time and money. Studies show that anywhere from 75% to 86% of Americans have stated that they've been involved philanthropically with a cause.[2] Charitable gifts given in 1999 by 58% of Americans amounted to almost one-third of the U.S. domestic federal budget—roughly 2% of the nation's income. What's more, charitable giving has become fashionable, rating a cover story in the July 24, 2000 issue of *Time* magazine along with prominent displays in other national news and financial magazines since then. It was also the subject of the first-ever White House conference on philanthropy. Gifts given during the time of the Asian tsunami, the Pakistani earthquake, and the hurricane disaster in New Orleans have been at unprecedented levels.

Similarly, the number of unpaid, volunteer workers in the nonprofit sector is striking, with volunteerism up even among young people. Some surveys indicate volunteering has risen 14 percentage points during the past 15 years, with roughly 58% of America's population having volunteered during the previous 12 months. And every year Americans donate around 15.5 billion hours of volunteer time, worth an estimated $4,239 billion in services.[3] Religious organizations, local schools, neighborhood organizations, and volunteer organizations based at one's workplace are the primary beneficiaries of this growth, with some civic organizations lagging behind in volunteer attraction.

In light of the relative "youth" of most nonprofit organizations (almost 70% have been registered during the past 30 years, while the nonprofit sector itself has grown almost 60% during the past two decades), the *reach* of some of the approximately one million nonprofit agencies is substantial. Representing almost 10% of this nation's workforce, the nonprofit world is apparent in almost every facet of life. However, alongside the positive developments and the humanizing effects the nonprofit world has upon society are strong marketplace indicators suggesting that changes are coming toward it in a nonlinear, sudden, and constant fashion.

Most importantly, these changes are being reflected in the increasing importance of donor values, the influence some donors want in organizational affairs on a day-to-day basis, and the manner by which some of their gifts are being made. Although this is not a new phenomenon, its effects are being felt today in almost all sectors of the nonprofit world. For example, according to a cover story in *The Chronicle of Philanthropy* a few years ago, the United Way faced the prospect of losing some of its market influence and strength in its traditional fund-raising practices because fewer workers were in offices (working instead at home and through flexible hours) and increasingly because United Way's donor base wanted to have a say in where their philanthropic dollars went (i.e., as opposed to relying on the United Way to allocate their gifts).[4] Similarly, *The Nonprofit Times* reported that the percentage of people opting out of charitable direct mail in categories ranging from health care to disaster relief began to outnumber those choosing to opt in.[5] In addition, hundreds of nonprofit organizations have reported receiving random donations during the past 36 months through their web sites from individuals they do not know.

Although some believe the nonprofit world and its member groups and associations have been characterized by tranquility and a lack of upheaval, nonprofit organizations are experiencing major changes and environmental pressures as they have for the past 20 years. These discontinuities have required many agencies to build stronger leadership and management teams and, in hundreds of cases, to change their marketing tactics.

During the 1960s and 1970s, nonprofit organizations saw rapid growth largely due to the infusion of funds the government pumped into the sector, particularly in health, education, research, and the arts. This picture changed in the 1980s during Reagan's presidency through severe government cutbacks; the sector was threatened again in 1995 as nonprofit funding sources came under the possibility of even more severe cutbacks when the House debated whether to replace social service and welfare programs with private volunteer charity. Though public sector funding decreased, non-profit organizations were often expected to shoulder even more of society's vexing social problems. As recently as the latter half of 2000, estate-tax repeals passed both houses of Congress (though later rejected by the administration), whose effect would likely have reduced some contributions to many charities.

The presence of so much affluence in America has had a tendency to cover up marketplace funding changes, and often it masks where in society, intervention is needed. While some donors are focusing resources and consolidating personal giving and volunteering, the rapid increase in nonprofit organizational creation during the past 30 years has typically not led to a duplication of services with some "lucky" individuals benefiting many times over, though the potential is clearly there. However, some societal changes are now so massive and rapid that they threaten to sweep away many of the foundational underpinnings the nonprofit world has stood on for dozens of years. These changes are more than an acceleration or the culmination point of existing trends; they are what authors Jim Taylor, Watts Wacker, and Howard Means described as a "fulcrum point in history," where many elements of change are converging, including

- The splintering of social, political, and economic organizations
- The collapse of producer-controlled markets
- A shift away from reason-based logic to chaos-based logic[6]

What will these changes mean for the nonprofit world? Clearly that world is susceptible to changes in its funding outlets as well as expectations society may have about how the sector should operate. A story about a man looking for lost money, often told at management seminars, is appropriate here:

> A man is on his knees under a street lamp, obviously looking for something under a well-lit area. A stranger passes by and asks the gentleman what he is doing. The gentleman replies that he is looking for his lost money. The stranger, wanting to be helpful, asks where the money was lost. "Over there," says the gentleman pointing away from the light. "Why, then, are you looking here instead of where you think your money is?" asks the stranger. "Because the light is better here," replies the gentleman.

As in the story, environmental changes could mean the preconceived expectations organizations have built their operations upon over the years may not work in chaotic conditions and may not be the only means by which they can achieve their goals. For some nonprofit organizations, new ways of operating are both plentiful and easily observable. In other institutions, talks of mergers with like-minded groups and the consolidation of provided services has become an important topic of conversation. Many agencies are also experimenting with board and governance models. For still others, textbook notions of a strong chief executive officer (coupled with a visionary management team whose members know where they are going at all times) guiding a unified work culture that is predictable and has an agreed-upon company vision may be the wrong metric against which some organizations should gauge their performance. This "institutional wisdom" may actually be dependent upon the economic and societal environments an agency encounters.

Similarly, some nonprofit leaders, in spite of their competencies as executives and managers, may not have a firm grasp of where their organizations will end up. These institutions may be leaders in their field and still not have an "institution-wide shared vision." Jeff McLinden, a vice president for the marketing and management consulting firm McConkey/Johnston, International suggests,

> For some organizations, the conventional rules of management and customer or donor interaction may not be the best way to prosper in some of the managerial or competitive situations they encounter. There is no one strategic management or marketing framework that is working for every nonprofit organization; there is "truth" in dozens of management and marketing approaches. Each nonprofit organization therefore must do business in a way that allows it to test the validity of the way chosen to approach the marketplace, what the medical world has called "evidence-based practice."[7]

Managing without Knowing the Future

Examples of nonprofit leaders having to manage without knowing how the American philanthropic future will impact their organizations abound. This is especially true in the explosive emergence of the Internet and the way it has changed the actual and mental geography of workers within many organizations. The Internet's presence has created for some a marketing and managerial quandary as to how their institutions should maximize it. Hundreds of nonprofit organizations have raced to create web sites and hire web teams without asking necessary prior tactical questions about their institution's objectives within its Internet usage. Consequently, most agencies in the United States today have created little more than vanity sites and, in the process, have allowed the customer or donor neither to be at the center of the site nor predisposed toward its cause. These same agencies have also failed to achieve the conversion ratios they had hoped for in converting the number of hits on their site to bona fide leads or gifts.

How does an agency harness the capabilities the Internet offers and simultaneously face the numerous issues and opportunities it presents? "Not knowing the future," agencies would be well served to first decide that simply bombarding their clientele with more direct mail, telemarketing, and expensive brochure creations while proclaiming that their institution is the best and the brightest is not the way to success. Media have become increasingly interactive, and stakeholders are exercising more control over what they give to or consume—how, when, and where. In some organizations with donors wanting more flexibility in the way they give and communicate, the Internet should be an option. For other groups, if target markets no longer respond positively to direct mail or telemarketing campaigns, the Internet may present a possible alternative. For still other groups dealing with stakeholders in the ages of 18 to 34, the Internet is this target group's primary source for information and entertainment. In each instance, the Internet may help reduce the interaction distance with institutions individuals express interest in and possibly create a stakeholder dialog as opposed to the monolog so many agencies currently impose upon their audiences.

In each of the foregoing cases of current or perceived future need, the Internet will prove helpful. Tactically, it may also afford organizations the opportunity to build new audience segments composed of like-minded e-givers (donors through the Internet), as well as changing how they give, when they give, and what they give to. Each new initiative and response consequently requires organizations to deal with staff and stakeholders differently than before. It is true that there have been widely reported success stories of Internet fund-raising and advocacy usage, including the American Red Cross, which reportedly raised over $1 million dollars for Balkan Relief in 1999; presidential hopefuls McCain's and later Dean's millions raised in their campaign bids; as much as 10% of the $1.5 billion given in relief donations after the terrorist actions in New York City; and the millions given during the Asian, Pakistani, and New Orleans' crises. This still does not mean the Internet is an immediate sure bet financially for all nonprofit organizations today.[8] The Internet has certainly represented a huge leap in information delivery for organizations. Will it do the same in the areas of fund-raising and transaction facilitation?

A nonprofit manager would have to look at additional concerns if he or she were required to make a reasonable decision regarding the deployment of resources for future Internet involvement. Excepting for highly vertical appeals or nationwide emergencies, the amount of money given charitably through the Internet has hovered at less than 2%. Of the more than $190 billion charitable donations given in 1999, about 1.2% of the donors did their giving through the Web.[9] This amount represents about 14 cents out of every $100 dollars given. Though comparatively small today, Internet giving potential may loom large for some nonprofit organizations in the future, especially given the outpouring of e-gifts after the 9/11 disaster and the tsunami, earthquake, and hurricane crises. "If the growth in Internet commerce is any indication, it could be tremendous," says independent sector senior analyst Michael T. McCormack.[10]

What "tremendous" might mean to development directors contemplating strategic decisions for the days ahead is hard to know. Certainly new tools are available to nonprofit marketers, including targeted e-mail lists, affiliated or consolidated giving sites like charitymall.com and Helping.org, and other interactive applications that allow shopping opportunities online (with a percentage of each purchase being earmarked for a particular charity). Each of these marketing options may seem attractive to an organization struggling to support its fund-raising efforts, especially if previous efforts have met with dwindling response rates in some parts of their customer and donor files.

Unfortunately, questions like these also come on top of both societal and environmental upheaval, as well as at times when some nonprofit organizations have been victims of scandal and mismanagement. According to Jan Masaoka, the executive director of The Support Center for Nonprofit Management, "We all know now about the loss of legitimacy of the nonprofit sector and the erosion of the moral high ground on which we used to stand."[11] As a consequence, an organization's "reason for being" is now more closely watched by both internal and external observers than ever before. Accordingly, many nonprofit organizations focus on short-term strategies they have current funds for, while negating long-term plans (that are often more needed in their causal arena).

Similarly, the outcomes nonprofit organizations produce on behalf of society and their own particular stakeholders, as well as the methods by which they produce them, are also being rethought by many of these same participants. Stories abound in print and in seminars of the "new philanthropists" who, having wealth and expertise within their own fields of endeavor, are now coming into the philanthropic world to "fix it" by dictating the terms of their involvement and the programs they are willing to fund. Some of these donors are generous and sincere and are making serious inroads in causal fields such as health care, education, and religion. In this process they are changing and improving the performance cultures of some of the organizations they're involved with. Other donors, however, may be celebrity seekers who are compromising the organization's philanthropic task for their own ends and in the process may have marginalized the seriousness of some causal needs.

One donor, in commenting on this new trend in philanthropic intervention and the philanthropists themselves, noted, "All they measure is what they have given rather than what the results are."[12]

In spite of some detractors and the ensuing uneasiness about the future, new infusions of donations and volunteers are needed in this

country more than ever. Second Harvest, the national organization
of food banks, projected that programs affiliated with its members
have provided food to minimally 25,970,000 "unduplicated"
clients in a year, mostly through kitchens and food pantries.[13] Of
the 12 million children under the age of three in the United States,
staggering numbers still live in conditions that threaten their lives.
One in four lives in poverty.[14]

There is still unprecedented need in the United States with the
inequities in our society continuing to get worse.

PHILANTHROPY IN THE LIGHT OF INSTITUTIONAL PRODUCTIVITY

Buried behind the stories of societal need is a massive problem. At its
core is the issue of philanthropic and organizational productivity
and the need for many organizations to rethink their best practices in
terms of operations.

Simply stated, the United States—and the world around it—is
drowning in a pool of human need. Of the six billion or so living in
the world presently, close to two billion could be classified as "in
trouble," with poor health and nutritional options. Eight hundred
million of these individuals are on the edge of starvation, with eight
million dying each year because they are too poor to survive.[15]
Intervention efforts on behalf of those in need are not enough to go
around. As a consequence, new, incredible pressures are being laid at
the feet of many nonprofit organizations to perform at levels
unheard of in the past.

For some institutional leaders feeling this burden, the need for
sustained and increased nonprofit productivity is increasingly
becoming an issue of the need to engage in organizational
transformation. Why is this?

The productivity-led recovery the United States experienced
during the second half of the 1990s and into the new millennium—a
recovery that the nonprofit world also derived some resource

benefit from—can be traced to the early 1970s, when many U.S. manufacturers, bloated with unwanted acquisitions and bureaucracies and being eclipsed competitively by many Asian-rim countries, realized how far they had moved from their core competencies. Institutions began and still continue to shed acquisitions and employees as the nation staggered from the technology and marketplace fallout it had experienced a few years earlier and then slowly recovered. Nonprofit organizations, again, are part of this wave, with some whose funding depended on the success of donors' stock portfolios still feeling the negative effects of gifts withheld during this time of economic transition. During the apogee of the high-tech fallout, it was not unusual for some nonprofit organizations to be depressed 30% or more in their donations as gifts dried up.

With approximately 70% of the nonprofit world having budgets under $500,000 a year and in the light of increasing competition and technological advances in how organizational processes can be delivered, many for-profit and not-for-profit industries have begun to rethink how they are going to convey their services in a global marketplace rife with "look-alike" products. In addition, rapid technological advances are reshaping how organizations operate, and this in turn is creating severe discontinuities throughout many nonprofit and for-profit corporate cultures. This genuinely new global economic era is forcing the need for change in how business is conducted in virtually all markets and sectors of society. Compounding this trend is the aging of 74 million baby boomers, given their requirements and demands for more service options and infrastructure choices.

Within the turbulent and unforgiving marketplace many organizations find themselves in, the need for a new, aggressive competitiveness, evolving business practices, and organizational structures is a nonstop process. As old industries are replaced by new engines of economic growth, this need is also seeping into the nonprofit world.

In fact, the need for change has seldom been so forcefully presented in parts of the nonprofit world as now. Not only is there an unprecedented demand for some organizations to become revitalized agents of change within their own spheres of civic responsibility, but they must also function with aggressive benefit to their mission, their stakeholders, and their bottom line. Many nonprofit institutions are desperate to answer these calls for change. Some, even with their donative resources on the increase, have not been able to keep pace with the commensurate demand for services. Other organizations are also being asked to do more in areas the federal government annexed in the 1960s but has retreated from now and serves less and less.

There are four broad areas of change affecting the nonprofit world today:

1. While the nonprofit sector is more professional than ever, those who fund and volunteer on behalf of organizations expect efficiency, customer consideration, and cutting-edge services. They are not shy in demanding superlative performance from the organizations they support. Nor are they shy in pushing themselves into the center of the agency's world. Often previously suppressed or marginalized at some institutions, donors, customers, and volunteers are taking active roles in the social, cultural, and intellectual dialogs many of these agencies have. When denied this chance for involvement, these individuals often leave the institution and take their support elsewhere. Nonprofit organizations must constantly balance the needs of these groups. As was noted by *The Economist* in 1998, the amateurishness of some nonprofit organizations has unfortunately led to an alarmingly high proportion of philanthropic giving sometimes going to gratifying people's egos rather than helping those in need.[16] On the opposite side of the coin, some nonprofit organizations have been criticized for looking too "Madison Avenue" in their marketing approach.

2. The foregoing issues have contributed negatively in the economic environment. Agencies with city or regionally based constituencies have often had to contend with a weakening of their local ties and drawing power as "glamorous" causes have effectively utilized the electronic media to convey their packaged appeals to households around the world. For many casual and would-be donors, these expertly packaged appeals on behalf of global or national crises are often more attractive and present an immediate option for individuals to express concern and act, rather than local issues, which are often poorly communicated and *hidden* from constituents by their lack of advertising or fund-raising budgets. It is not unusual to have individuals in a community not know where their local food pantry is located, but to be able to recognize international relief agencies by name that advertise around favorite television or cable shows these same individuals watch.

3. In addition, the worlds of business and third-sector institutions are colliding more frequently, and nonprofit organizations are increasingly being benchmarked against their for-profit neighbors. Occurring with some rapidity through the ability of organizations to radically upgrade their information technology systems at affordable prices, this "collision" has also increased pressure on organizations to perform with attention to the bottom line. This effect is, in turn, forcing some organizations to move away from a "marketing pre-culture" (where marketing issues are only talked about and not engaged) to a true "marketing culture." Unfortunately, many nonprofit organizations are simply not prepared to compete in today's aggressive world. This can be evidenced in a number of ways—an organization may experience a lack of competent marketing staff, or it may engage in fund-raising strategies that are no longer viable, or most commonly, it may

have an inadequate marketing budget to make any difference through its promotional programs.

4. Point three indicates the negative side of not having enough competent people; there is a silver lining in this situation as well. Having a lack of competent internal staff to draw from has caused many agencies to seek help elsewhere, and they are benefiting today from the advice, participation, and change insurgency a new generation of corporate layoffs, key volunteers, and early retirees from the corporate sector are bringing into their everyday organizational lives. It is not surprising to say that it is people who are helping to shape the new world of philanthropy. People have always been at the center of nonprofit life. What is surprising is the numbers of individuals, often from the for-profit sector, who are serving as revitalizing agents of change through their volunteerism or willingness to take reduced salaries in order to serve on behalf of a nonprofit organization.

Four brief stories highlight this trend.

REAL-WORLD EXAMPLES

Forbes.com reported the story of Edward Morgan, who after serving two decades in the General Electric corporate sector, came to a midtown Manhattan mission for men and women battling drugs and alcohol. Along with revamping all of the management systems and stopping the financial hemorrhaging, Morgan increased the donor revenue stream, off-loaded organizational sacred cows, and ran the mission in the black. In addition, he increased the career training the mission offered to make an even longer-lasting impact in the lives of those he serves.*

Al Wunderlich, 68, managed a 27-person staff as head of Anheuser-Busch's global tax division before he retired in 1996.

As the director of the Franklin Neighborhood Community Association in Belleville, Illinois, he sometimes mopped floors, along with helping the nonprofit abandon some of its hidebound practices.[†]

John Wood served along with his wife as directors of Heritage Home, a home for unwed mothers who would be destitute on the street were it not for the services provided by the Home. Before he came to Heritage Home, John ran a $100 million company that made extensive use of assembly-line technology. Having taken early retirement he used those honed skills to create synergies in the lives of young women who needed to figure out how to reengage with society.[**]

Don Mercer came to Eagle Village—a sprawling campus for kids at risk—and used his Pentagon experience in scenario planning and tactics to successfully put the Village in the black. He upgraded or rebuilt almost all of its facilities and substantially benchmarked its services at a higher level.[††]

[*] Adams, Susan, "Corporate Communion," Forbes.com, May 5, 2000.
[†] Tanz, Jason with Theodore Spencer, "Candy Striper, My Ass!" *Fortune*, August 14, 2000, p. 160.
[**] From the personal client files of Barry McLeish.
[††] Ibid.

Each of the individuals brought skills from the corporate or military sector to help them manage and succeed in the nonprofit world. In the process, they demonstrated that skills learned and used in one sector can be transferable and helpful in another.

Unfortunately, in spite of these inspiring stories and many others like them, some myths permeate the nonprofit marketplace that are hard to dispel and therefore, though imprecise and emotional, have a dampening effect on the performance and productivity of some organizations. In this time of frequent radical marketplace change, new skills borrowed and learned from *outside* the nonprofit arena may become more valuable once taken *inside* organizations. However, many management principles handed down within nonprofit institutions are inimical to innovation. Consequently, some organizations, unless they become open to innovations in how they operate, will continue to have their hands tied by the managerial myths that seem pervasive. There are four popular managerial myths plaguing the nonprofit world today.

First: You Must Be a Large Organization to Make a Difference

This first myth seems to have the longest tenure and causes the most angst. There is a sense often present at nonprofit management and fund-raising training events that ultimately a handful of large mega-nonprofit organizations are going to carve up the service world, and in so doing, they are going to parcel out doing good deeds among themselves. This notion comes naturally as nonprofit leaders at every level and in every type of organization are repeatedly exposed, along with the larger for-profit business community, to the idea that the only way to deal with competitors in this world is to beat them at their own game and become large enough to be impervious to their threats. John Kenneth Galbraith said as much when he wrote *The New Industrial State* more than 30 years ago and suggested that the world would be run by large corporations. Large companies gained efficiencies in their operations, and efficiency became *the* competency that was hard for competitors to overcome. However, "large" has not turned out to be the dominant model in the non-profit world, nor is it necessarily a critical criterion organizations must have in order to help those they seek to serve. One need only look at the means by which communities offer help to those in need to see that this is true. Most shelters, food pantries, nonprofit schools, counseling services, hotlines, and volunteer forces work through local initiatives and make a difference at the local level. While it is sometimes hard to assess these initiatives through the lenses of productivity, it is not hard to assess the pragmatic effects on the lives of individuals touched by efforts at helping at the local level.

Large or small, each model carries with it operational liabilities and strengths, and neither can be said to be the perfect operational system. Large nonprofit organizations often make a profound difference, and a number of them, particularly those that have a chance to work throughout the nation or around the world, bring significant resources to bear upon particular issues and do tremendous good. However, small nonprofit organizations have some tactical advantages. For example, they have none of the fixed costs of larger institutions. Further, they often become crucial to a local community's safety net for those in need. The advent of technology also allows them to data-mine customer and donor bases that were once the province of larger nonprofit firms. Additionally, small institutions typically have the ability to experiment with new responses to social needs in a quicker and more immediate fashion than many larger, managerially bloated organizations. In addition, because of their ability to respond immediately to marketplace initiatives, smaller organizations can react more quickly to change their service and marketing approaches where appropriate, whereas a lack of support for new initiatives in a larger organization is often masked because of the large number of programs and the distance between the organization and its constituents.

Second: Only Well-Known Organizations Can Raise Money and Provide Excellent Service

Tied closely to the first myth is the idea that only a few, well-known, elite nonprofit organizations, supported by their recognizable brand names and large marketing and fund-raising machines, will gradually overshadow all other competitors. This is a dominant theme echoed by many nonprofit executives in light of hyper-marketplace competition. What these same nonprofit leaders often do not realize is that large fund-raising efforts can simply gloss over regional differences in favor of exploiting economies of scale by asking for the same cause in the same way wherever they are. For example, this is the normative behavior for many direct-mail–driven organizations. Although these same organizations may achieve some economies of scale, treating all fundraising prospects as if they were the same can have serious drawbacks in tightly knit communities.

Comparing one's organization against a better-known competitor often ignores reasons why some individuals make philanthropic choices that are local or regional in nature. An individual may feel marginalized by gender, race, or physical handicap and identify with a cause that does not embrace the dominant culture. Some may have stronger value alignment with lesser-known organizations that seem more personal in their approach. Further, a man or woman's financial gift or voluntary act may seem to be more appreciated by staff and others alike in lesser-known or smaller organizations that willingly dote on their donors, volunteers, and customers.

Consider the example of individuals who send their sons and daughters to camp each summer. Decisions like these are often based on criteria other than the name recognition of the institution or its reputation. They may depend as much as the parents' need to see their child experience rites of passage similar to their own at a particular age. The action of sending a child to camp may be tied to personal parental values, interests, or vision of what their child needs to experience rather than the actual or perceived competency of the institution.

Comparatively speaking, there are only a handful of very well-known, nationwide causes and institutions that are a part of the third sector. Many of these large, global causes must often decentralize their operations in different ways to take advantage of local resources. Not doing so can easily become a mistake in marketing tactics. Even so, local causal initiatives almost always have a service or marketing niche that larger concerns have a hard time imitating. Their proximity allows them to serve customers, donors, and volunteers in a way that other, larger organizations can't. In speaking about caring for customers and donors, Tom Bisset, general manager of WRBS in Baltimore, notes "all relationships are ultimately local."[17] Perhaps for many causes, so is service, volunteering, and fund-raising. Smaller nonprofit organizations may be better positioned to take advantage of tomorrow's opportunities than their larger neighbors.

Third: Many Americans View Nonprofit Organizations Differently Today

From an economist's point of view, a donor to a nonprofit organization is a purchaser of services. For some donors, the fundamental difference between their purchasing a service and a product you or I might buy from a commercial outlet is simply that in the charitable act, donors seldom see the services in action because they are delivered to a third party. As such, donors are often at risk in the transaction because they have no easy way to determine whether the services they purchased were rendered as promised and expected. The organization in turn, hopes the donors will trust that they will keep their word and deliver what was promised. While this is usually the case, sometimes the donor's trust in the organization isn't warranted. These unfortunate instances contribute to the mistrust some individuals have regarding nonprofit agencies.

This mistrust is compounded by another prevalent condition. When individuals give a financial gift, it is usually labeled as a "charitable gift." Unfortunately, labeling these philanthropic actions as charity often generates a misleading notion. The word *charity* often gives rise to images of helping people who are homeless, desperate for food, or in dire circumstances. Today, charitable acts on behalf of individuals may achieve different goals—for example:

- Gifts going to a local church or service club may more directly benefit members than those in need who are outside the church or club's sphere of influence.

- A university donation may pay for staff salaries to maintain excellent staff, with only a fraction earmarked for those who cannot afford higher education.

Philanthropic realities such as these have a cumulative effect upon society and can impact the way some individuals view charities.

In addition, because America has achieved unprecedented material prosperity and personal freedom during the past 20 years, what were once luxuries in our society have now become necessities. For some, attaining these freedoms has not necessarily made for a better public. For others, however, achieving these freedoms has created the expectation that an individual must control as many aspects of the entire donative transaction as possible to ensure that the organization does not succumb to providing lesser services than what was promised.

For still others, notions of service and care for those less fortunate—concerns about larger societal issues such as racial harmony, a clean environment, safe cities, better educational systems, and other shared moral imperatives—have been replaced by attitudes of blame and intolerance for social ills. Rather than addressing societal concerns in communities or taking a personal approach to them, these individuals now believe others should solve them.

This stance is compounded by widespread feelings in society that some of today's issues are simply intractable. While most in this country do not suffer from terrible living conditions, no health insurance, a lack of food, or diseases that go untreated, nevertheless there is a feeling by many that these problems will never be corrected and are simply beyond the collective desire and ability of society to solve.

Given feelings of disappointment with self and society over the failure to solve these crises, compounded by an unending desire for material consumption fed by a capitalism that long ago stopped being compassionate, many people increasingly have little patience for those who cannot cope nor succeed. Writes national columnist Robert J. Samuelson about the face of American capitalism, "It is less protective and more predatory. It no longer promises ultimate security or endless entitlement. Instead, it preaches the inevitability of change, implying that change is often cruel."[18]

Fourth: Experience Is All That Counts

If there were no marketplace changes to speak of, this statement would most likely be true. People who have had the longest careers and have been around the most, as well as having had the most institutional experience, would have a decided advantage over those who possessed fewer experiences or had served fewer years. However, for a third-sector organization, avoiding marketplace changes today is usually more a matter of sheer luck than anything else.

Remembering when the pace of change was slower, some nonprofit executives see what is happening outside their organizations as being independent of what their institutions need to choose to do operationally. Rather than modifying how they operate or promoting their causal products in a different manner or changing their infrastructure systems and procedures, these individuals operate based on how they wished the world around them would operate. Striving instead for balance and equilibrium in order to create a type of changeless organizational orthodoxy, these directors "make no changes." Should they accomplish this organizational goal, they then tend to lose the courage to offload organizational entities that represent outmoded ways of thinking. Instead, outmoded ideas grow to be organizationally sacrosanct, becoming a type of organizational truth and meta-narrative for operating.

Challenging what an organization holds as experiential truth is a continual process, and should it encounter some idea or "truth" that is no longer helpful or realistic, an organization must learn to discard it. London-based nonprofit marketing consultant Redina Kolaneci suggests, "We must always look at our assumptions about how something should work. Are they still true? If not, why not? What is it in our belief systems that we must change?"[19]

To not do what Redina Kolaneci suggests is to ignore the notion that organizations are complex systems that out of necessity, must interact with those who are "outside," exchanging ideas and mutually influencing each other. To undertake these actions enables institutions to help avoid wrong thinking, abandoning rather than defending what went on previously.

As conditions change, organizational models, along with the experience and wisdom they once represented, may not hold up anymore, as in the following examples:

- For years, city rescue missions ignored the trend that the homeless population was not exclusively composed of men but had become heavily skewed toward women, many of them with children. Once this was grasped as a statistical reality, new training had to be brought into many missions to adequately deal with the issues women and children brought with them, to say nothing of the need for new living and housing quarters to accommodate this new clientele.

- Religious organizations that send missionaries through deputational (i.e., personalized support) fund raising have had to contend with rising costs in foreign countries, thereby threatening their funding model. For a family of four Americans to go as a missionary family to Japan and secure adequate housing and education for their children can easily cost the sending organization more than $100,000 per year. The deputational funding model (sometimes known as "personal support raising," in use for years) of going from church to church or diocese to diocese to ask for funds simply is inadequate as a strategy for many missionary families going overseas, given the amount of money these individuals must often raise. A new way of achieving an organization's financial needs must be explored.

How? The need for a new mind-set in the way nonprofit organizations operate with stakeholders and with other non-profit agencies is required as never before; this is the subject of Chapter 2.

▨ NOTES

1. O'Neill, Michael, The Third America *(San Francisco: Jossey-Bass, 1989)*, p. 16.
2. Greenfeld, Karl Taro, *"A New Way of Giving,"* Time, *July 24, 2000, p. 48.* See also *"Vertis Customer Focus 2003,"* Chronicle of Philanthropy, *October 16, 2003, p. 30.*
3. Ladd, Everett Carl, The Ladd Report *(New York: The Free Press, 1999)*, p. 62. Eggar, Robert *(with Howard Yoon)*, Begging for Change *(New York: HarperBusiness, 2004), p. 45.*
4. *"United Ways Seek a New Identity,"* The Chronicle of Philanthropy, *March 9, 2000, p. 1.*
5. *"Donors Now Opting-Out of Mailings,"* The Nonprofit Times, *March 1, 2000, p. 1.*
6. Taylor, Jim, Watts Wacker, and Howard Means, The 500 Year Delta *(New York: HarperBusiness, 1997), p. xiv.*
7. *Personal conversation with Jeff McLinden of McConkey/Johnston in Atlanta at the Christian Stewardship Conference, September 28, 2000.*
8. *Presentation at the Christian Stewardship Conference in Atlanta on October 1, 2000.*
9. Caruso, Iyna Bart, *"Celebrity Charity Goes Cyber,"* American Way, *p. 102.*
10. Ibid., *p. 102.*
11. Masaoka, Jan, *"Opening Address,"* in Giving to the Future: Philanthropy in the Twenty-First Century *(San Francisco: Community Foundations of the San Francisco Bay Area, 1998), p. 9.*
12. Greenfeld, Karl Taro, *"A New Way of Giving,"* Time, *July 24, 2000, p. 57.*
13. Shore, Bill, The Cathedral Within *(New York: Random House, 1999), p. 8.*
14. Poppendieck, Janet, Sweet Charity? *(New York: Viking Penguin, 1998), p. 3–4.*
15. Kluger, Jeffrey and Andrea Dorfman, *"The Challenges We Face,"* Time, *August 26, 2002. "The End of Poverty," excerpted from* The End of Poverty, *Jeffrey Sachs,* Time, *March 14, 2005.*
16. The Economist, *May 30, 1998.*

17. *From the personal client files of Barry McLeish.*
18. *Samuelson, Robert J., The Good Life and Its Discontents (New York: Times Books, 1995), p. 120.*
19. *Personal conversation with Redina Kolaneci in Colorado Springs, October 2003.*

▨ REFERENCES

Burns, James Macgregor, *Leadership* (New York: Harper Torchbooks, 1978).

Galbraith, John Kenneth, *The New Industrial State* (New York: Mentor, 1971).

CHAPTER 2

The Need for a New Mind-Set

There is a story told at seminars about Albert Einstein, who, as a professor, was known to give the same test questions to students year after year. When questioned about this behavior by his secretary, he noted that though the questions were indeed the same, the answers often changed year by year. When I started out in marketing and development, the strategic and tactical issues I faced, as well as the questions other nonprofit executives faced, were substantially different from those our successors faced 15, 10, and even 5 years later, though the questions were often the same. Obviously, there are reoccurring issues every nonprofit executive seems to confront—"Are we helping those we need to?," "Can we achieve an advantage in the marketplace?," and the like.

Today however, successful nonprofit executives must deal with two strategic issues in a better way than the competition:

1. Is the way we are operating and handling our institution's affairs allowing us to achieve the goals for which it was created—whether that be the number of people served, dollars raised, or volunteers recruited—or must we change our infrastructure in order to achieve these goals and keep faith with our stakeholders?

2. How are we going to succeed?

Christopher Columbus, for example, failed to answer these two questions correctly in light of his mission to sail to China, in spite of the fact that he discovered a new world. Was Columbus a success or a failure? For some answering this question, herein lies a paradox. The same paradox and difficulty often occurs in discussing nonprofit leadership.

Developing answers to the question of achieving agency goals can be a rather daunting task in the light of the opinions many management theorists, authors, and others have expressed regarding the role of the nonprofit strategist. In the minds of many of these social critics, the job of a strategist is inherently ambiguous, because performance measures used in the for-profit world (such as profit measures) do not work as well in the nonprofit environment, where the function of the organization is theoretically to contribute to the greater good, as in the following example.

REAL-WORLD EXAMPLES

For the past 10 years, a camp on the East Coast has run programs for young people in a prescribed manner according to its religious culture. This culture mandates what types of religious delivery systems need to be in place, how campers are to be taught, and who can teach, and it suggests appropriate daily activities for the campers. Money for the operations of the camp is typically given by individuals from within the religious community along with fees collected from campers. For the years 1996 through 2001, the operating margins of the camp have declined precipitously, even though some other camps in the same geographical region have grown financially. The reason for this decline is thought by the leadership of the camp to be due principally to the defection of donors, presumably to other causes.*

*From the personal client files of Barry McLeish.

Though there are many questions that could be asked in light of this example, perhaps the most critical question is, "Is the leadership mismanaging the camp?" In answering this question, some individuals might note that apart from hints suggesting operational difficulties, one could answer, "Not necessarily." However, there does seem to be a movement away from the traditionally imposed culture of the camp on the part of campers, customers, and various donor groups. By implication, there also seems to be a realignment of their evaluation of the organization. The way the camp currently is operating, with little managerial risk, a status-quo approach to its environment, and almost no programmatic innovation during the past five years puts it at a competitive disadvantage with camps that are changing some of their operational approaches to reflect new customer expectations.

A different example of misalignment between an organization and its stakeholders comes from a nonprofit institution operating within a different causal industry yet facing similarly complex issues, as in the following example.

REAL-WORLD EXAMPLES

This institution for troubled young people has existed for the past five years with a relatively flat budget. Neither state subsidies nor infrequent attempts at fund-raising have increased its budget substantially. Operated both as a "holding tank" for youthful offenders and as a center for their rehabilitation, this institution has seen a steady decline in its importance among critical stakeholder groups, including donors, volunteers, and state agencies. Operating in a chronically understaffed situation with the net effect of under-serving the young people entrusted to its care, the institution has maintained its balanced budget annually by cutting staff, freezing wages, and deferring maintenance.*

*From the personal client files of Barry McLeish.

Is this agency being mismanaged? Again, some might suggest the organization is simply at a bad spot in the road. However, the agency is experiencing movement in the way individuals respond to its financial needs, which may reflect a shift in values from some of these same donative communities. It is also seeing a possible shift in values from some legislators who have traditionally acted as funders to the agency. The business design for this institution is no longer working as well as it needs to. If it does not take corrective action and change its organizational approach soon, this agency for troubled youth might face the possibility of going out of business.

These two organizations are having the same type of disjointed organizational experience many readers can relate to, that of driving their car in a rainstorm while the radio announcer proclaims it is a sunny day outside. Both sets of organizational leaders are making the mistake of being in the midst of marketplace changes and not responding to them. In each example, the way the organizations once conducted their business affairs is no longer working as well as is needed in the economic environments they now find themselves in. Adrian Slywotzky, a founding partner of Corporate Decisions, writes, "It is widely acknowledged that products go through cycles from growth through obsolescence. It is not as well recognized that business designs also go through cycles and reach economic obsolescence."[1]

Not only are customer and donor values shifting in the examples, but so are the service and donative priorities of those funding and supporting the organizations mentioned. Does the new path these donors and supporters seem to be following mean they've stopped giving away money? Have they decided against philanthropic pursuits? Most likely not. It seems more likely to assume the core values of donating money and allocating support by the individuals in question is in the process of being transferred to other organizations that now have taken the place of the original causes first supported.

Why do individuals frequently reallocate their giving priorities? The answer can often be found in the way organizations engage or do not engage their customers, donors, and volunteers. Unless there is a seamless web of reciprocal collaboration and interaction centered on the institution, individuals may choose to partner with someone else. Donors and volunteers may reallocate their giving or volunteer efforts after seeing or negatively experiencing the way their resources were being used by an organization, or hearing criticism about the way in which the organization was serving those it was supposed to help. Some individuals might also reallocate their giving as a result of being thanked inappropriately for their financial or volunteer support, or they may feel embarrassed by the way the organization communicates and reports its activities to the public. In each instance, a type of value is created—or is not created—for those who support the organization.

As can be seen in the examples cited previously, the business design each organization had been using no longer allowed it to deliver maximum service and value to its key audiences. In these instances, the business design and winning strategic formula that may have worked in the past are now making the organizations victims of their own success. Strategies that once shaped these organizations have become prisons that do not allow them to succeed in a changing world. As a consequence, the leadership of these organizations, trusting that predictable maps and old controls are still applicable even in times of marketplace change, become vulnerable to competitors who bring a different type of competitive strategy into their operations. These unchanging nonprofit institutions easily find themselves no longer in alignment with their key stakeholders' wants and needs. In most cases, the leadership of these organizations has at some point stopped asking the questions posed at the beginning of this chapter:

1. Is the way we are operating and handling our institution's affairs allowing us to achieve the goals for which it was

created, or must leadership change the infrastructure in order to achieve these goals and keep faith with the stakeholders?

2. How are we going to succeed?

To answer these questions correctly typically requires an organization first to work through four issues, which are described in the following subsections.

First: The Need for a New Managerial and Marketing Mind-Set

The marketing efforts of many third-sector institutions are being forced to undergo a major restructuring for one simple reason. These organizations are not achieving their corporate missions in a manner and time frame that seems satisfactory. The result is that many institutions are moving from a set culture and a reliance on stereotyped fund-raising approaches that sometimes were coupled with a disregard for their supportive constituents toward an acknowledgment of their need for additional help and a different approach. This results in a new emphasis on organizational collaboration and individual donor, volunteer, and member fulfillment. Some in the field have mistakenly called this cultural change "donor-driven philanthropy," implying that we have moved from a philanthropic world where there were agreed-on roles for donors, volunteers, customers, and organizations they were interested in to a new world where, philosophically, stakeholders are pitted against the institutions they support.

This has never been the case. In fact, researchers in the philanthropic arena have seen this shift in donor choice and the resulting need for donor and customer personal fulfillment taking place over time, with thousands of enlightened institutions already sensing the need for collaboration with stakeholders as a way to fulfill their corporate missions.[2]

Regardless of how it is labeled, there is clearly a movement away from the overly simplistic models of philanthropy and marketing that governed nonprofit organizational actions for years, to a stronger inclusion of previously neglected human factors, often individualized in nature. Along with this movement of transition and transformation has been the realization by some nonprofit leaders that their personnel, fund-raising, and marketing management systems were often structurally ineffective.

REAL-WORLD EXAMPLE

I was asked to speak to a new client's board of directors. Only 3 of the 12 board members showed up at the regularly scheduled board meeting. Later, as I met with the embarrassed director, I found that the organization for years had operated in an environment where only a few people seemed to truly pursue its goals. Within the organization there was a distinct lack of both performance management and a marketing culture. Donors seemed to be valued more for their money than for who they were. Program staff refused to have anything to do with marketing and public-relations issues, and the number of volunteers helping the organization had dwindled to nearly zero.

Theirs was a dysfunctional organizational culture in which there seemed little opportunity to craft a carefully nuanced environment that donors, customers, and volunteers would want to be a part of. The language of marketing and management was used and talked about, but both seemed more artificially contrived than authentic. In particular, during the course of the board meeting, aspects of an organizational marketing culture were noticeably absent, including mission language, the expressed values of the organization, and a concern for the opinions and actions of volunteers and donors.

While all nonprofit organizations are dependent on systems, not all are successful in managing them. A key difference between the successful and the unsuccessful ones can often be found in their organizational and marketing cultures.

Do organizations operating this way survive for long? Surprisingly, many do, often because of a pattern of repeated emotional solicitations and aggressive fund-raising, though usually at declining levels of response and commensurate service, until the organizations either transform themselves or the leadership finds it difficult to stay operational.

Many leaders have become aware of these structural obstacles to renewal and change. Originally designed to be rigid and impersonal and to keep as many as possible from decision-making and shared power, some nonprofit bureaucratic systems are now being seen as structures that need to be dealt with and changed, not simply taken for granted. Additionally, this perspective has taken on ethical overtones for many would-be change agents. As individuals inside and outside bureaucracies note, some structures that have been in place for long periods of time now reflect a type of arrogance, power, privilege, interest, and influence that has become legitimized in the marketplace and that operationally mitigates against the notion of community. Because of their permanence within some organizations, which contributes in many cases to their presumed "managerial rightness" and rationality, changing these systems of leadership and bureaucracy is a hard task.

Bringing about change can create periods of flux, uncertainty, and experimentation, and this in turn affects how supporters and institutions talk to each other. Shared beliefs between stakeholders and the organizations they support often begin to lack cohesion and consensus regarding the direction the organization is taking and easily break down. Institutional communication between the two parties becomes background noise as both begin to feel the lack of similar beliefs, ideas, and actions.

A third nonprofit example tells a different institutional story.

REAL-WORLD EXAMPLES

This organization has enjoyed an average 13% growth rate over the past five years with both a steadily increasing population being served and a growing donor base. Its volunteers and its donor base regularly interact with the institution's leadership and vice versa through formal and informal methods. Stakeholders are interested in and concerned about the quality of care the institution provides those it serves. Polled repeatedly and interacted with routinely, stakeholders have the chance to let the organizational leadership know their opinions. Knowing these opinions allows the leadership team to build its business operations and marketing design around the reality of stakeholder priorities. This also allows programmatic leadership to develop cutting-edge programs for the population served and, commensurately, allows donors and volunteers to have trust in the way the mission is carried out.*

*From the personal client files of Barry McLeish.

This organization operates in a reality defined by both itself and its stakeholders. Almost all successful nonprofit agencies operate within this type of reality, characterized by three operational elements that exist side by side with each other on a daily basis:

- There is a strong stakeholder connection.

- This connection in turn feeds the organization's ability to innovate programs or reinvest in existing programs that are mandated and supported by stakeholders.

- Being connected with critical individuals in one's database allows an institution to know how to serve them through strengthening or redeployment of resources in the agency's infrastructure.

Unfortunately, some nonprofit leaders deal with their surrounding environment in a manner that assumes the environment is one way, when the reality is quite different. Consequently, it is easy for an organization to move out of alignment with those who support it. However, by listening carefully to those they work with and to other critical audiences, an organization can make sure it is dealing with the right issues and pulling as much as possible in the same direction as its stakeholders.

Equal in importance to listening, a nonprofit organization must also ensure that the marketing tactics used with one generation or audience are not now forced upon new prospective supporters who have little interest in how things used to be. Each causal product generation is different from the both previous one and the one that will follow. Successful organizations discern the priorities and communication styles of their stakeholders and set their marketing standards anew in a manner that meets their approval, as shown in the following example.

REAL-WORLD EXAMPLES

A nonprofit organization has for years recruited college students for its summer work in the same way: booths at job fairs, flashy brochures, radio ads, posters displayed in key campus areas, as well as relying on its reputation to draw collegians in. With recruitment off substantially, the organization recreated its web site and moved to an Internet strategy that promoted dialog around the typical questions collegians have regarding salary, housing, days off, and other issues key to their decision whether to work for the organization. The institution's strategy paid off handsomely, and in one season the staffing decline was reversed.*

*From the personal client files of Barry McLeish.

Second: The Need for System-Wide Alignment

How does an organization ensure that the individuals associated with it are moving in roughly the same direction, and vice versa? Is it important to do so?

The best place to start is to first ascertain whether an organization is internally focused or externally focused. To put the question another way, "Does the nonprofit organization care to understand and pay close attention to its stakeholders, market changes, competitors, and industry-specific trends, or not?" To answer positively is to be externally focused, poised to respond to evolving volunteer and donor needs and preferences. To answer in the negative is to become organizationally insular, to have a slower response time to marketplace changes, and to find one's agency often at a competitive disadvantage with causally similar institutions. Rather than viewing the shifting marketplace as a problem to be dealt with, successful nonprofit agencies see the marketplace as their source of growth. Within their organizational cultures, priority is given to gathering and analyzing marketplace data in order to make strategic decisions. Close attention is paid to this process.

The notion of "paying close attention to stakeholders" is an important one. As organizations grow and their environments change, institutional leaders often have to revise the business and marketing designs they operate with so there is a fit between design and environment. Without such adjustments, organizations can lack focus and fit with their environment and, as a consequence, lose effectiveness. Working to create alignment allows organizational partners, friends, and employees to look at mutually agreed-on purposes to be shared by each party. This in turn helps create a self-reinforcing culture with the desire to integrate institutional resources to achieve mutually agreed-on purposes. In a previous example, growth and transformation occurred as stakeholders inside and outside the organization intersected with each other and became aware of each other's values, actions, and lived experiences.

The lack of alignment can become painfully clear to an institution, as is shown in the following example.

REAL-WORLD EXAMPLES

An organization working with the poor and indigent spends most of its donated dollars providing food, shelter, clothing, and personal counseling to those it works with. Having decided organizationally that they should go a step further in helping those in need, they decided to buy a profit-making enterprise and train the people in its programs to work within the newly purchased company. Having worked out the tax implications and governance issues internally, the organization stood poised to use donated dollars to buy the new company. The institution then developed a public-relations program to present the purchase and the new program to the public, and it did so with lots of fanfare. The response by the public and its donors was subdued at best. For some donors, the possible purchase of a for-profit enterprise represented a betrayal of sorts. Other supporters questioned the organization's ability to manage this new function in a cost-effective way and wondered whether it fit within the agency's mission. It became painfully clear that had the organization talked to its constituents prior to buying the company, it might have been saved from an embarrassing incident and might have been able to reverse the process.*

*From the personal client files of Barry McLeish.

Because most nonprofit organizations must, by their very nature, walk cooperatively with other stakeholder groups in order to find funding and support, mutual support can lead to a series of rational actions that are cooperative in nature. In the first two examples concurrence would take root culturally because stakeholder research was mandated and budgeted for within the institution, allowing questions to be asked of the organization itself and its constituent groups, with the answers to these questions provided with due seriousness by the organization. In the third example, there was no attempt to listen to the constituency. Action was taken unilaterally by the organization with dire consequences.

As important as it is that people work together across personal and organizational boundaries, it is equally important that they work on agreed-on critical agendas. Critical agendas are often arrived at by donors, customers, and institutional representatives as each party is heard face-to-face, eliminating as many communication barriers as possible. Hearing and understanding allow an organization to know the values of its supportive constituents and in turn, to be able to create and deliver programs that are appreciated and, in some cases, mandated by donors and customers. Peer groups, listening conferences, e-mail discussion groups, sampling research, and inferential surveys are tools many nonprofit groups use to try to understand their constituents.

Walking cooperatively and in alignment with individuals also means asking how one's own institution can enhance the donor or volunteer experience at every level of encounter with the organization. To desire to do so is often easier said than done, but it is crucial to the experience people have with an organization they are interested in. To choose not to walk cooperatively with stakeholders often means organizational ideas of retaining donors and volunteers for longer periods of time are put in jeopardy. It is important for agency leaders not to delude themselves regarding this issue. Stakeholders are not typically spineless beings who can be chronically misled. They vote and do so with their time, energies, financial gifts, and actions.

Retaining an individual's loyalty to an organization, along with the creation of value for the same donor, customer, or volunteer is crucial to any successful, long-lasting nonprofit organization, and that should be the ultimate aim of any alignment strategy. Customer, donor, or volunteer preference and loyalty will come to a nonprofit organization if the institution takes the time to do the following three alignment activities well:

1. The organization must develop concrete, measurable approaches to its work that can be easily demonstrated to supportive constituents. For example, it might state "Our goal this year is to create 12 campus affiliates."

2. The institution must spend considerable amounts of time talking about the collaborative aspects of the work it undertakes. The evidenced culture to stakeholders is one of collaboration and partnership. For example, the organization in its direct-mail copy uses "You and I" language. In the organizational newsletter as well as on its web site there are feature stories about key volunteers and how their contribution affects the organization positively. Similarly, at public events, the chief executive officer goes out of his or her way to recognize stakeholder help.

3. The institution must spend time trying to understand what it is that their donors and customers value and how well the institution is delivering this value. For example, the organization funds a statistically valid constituent survey every two years to determine attitudes toward the organization and its work. In addition, during the course of any year the chief executive officer stages two listening conferences where various stakeholders are invited in to discuss the issues the organization is facing and dealing with.

Unfortunately, most U.S. corporations lose their customers within five years, half their employees in four, and half their investors in less than one year.[3] Reversing this trend and gaining donor, customer, and volunteer loyalty enables a nonprofit organization to increase the net revenue available to it to invest in its mission.

The benefits of alignment, loyalty, and cooperative action by donors and volunteers can be measured easily over time in three important ways:

1. The return (or the "profit or income" generated) on the marketing or development investment is almost always greater than its cost.

2. The cost to the organization of securing the partnership with individuals is typically eclipsed by the dollars given and the investment back into the organization on the part of those involved.

3. The percentage of donated dollars a person gives to the organization or the percentage of time an individual spends volunteering in an organization as compared with other organizations that fail to spend time in alignment activities is typically greater.

The first measure, the return on marketing and development investment, shows the organization how much it is spending to acquire new donors or volunteers. This type of calculation is most often seen in direct-mail campaigns; unfortunately, it is not seen as much in analyzing other solicitation media. As an organization becomes more skilled in acquiring donors and volunteers, its return on investment increases, as is true of the second measure, the cost of selling. This simply shows the revenue that comes into an organization that is reclaimable after its selling or fund-raising cycle and expenses. The third measure is the percentage of money each donor gives to an organization—in other words, the "loyalty" a donor displays on behalf of the organization.

A marketing department still must be concerned with the organization's cash flow in its day-to-day operation, but it must also look at the long-term value the organization has vis-à-vis its stakeholders. Cash flows rise and fall depending on the actions the marketing and development units of an institution take. However, these actions also have a lot to do with intangible factors, particularly the credibility the organization has with its donor and volunteer relationships and the strength these relationships evidence. This might be called institutionally its "return on value" or its "return on credibility."

To achieve a return on credibility or value and to be able to take cooperative action with individuals takes us to the third point: A an institution must also know what its mission is and what it is not. Not being entirely honest about this issue usually means the organization has the illusion it can be all things to all people. However, it is the affirmed values an organization holds with its constituents that defines what it is in business to do. An organization must know what causal business its key stakeholders think it is in. Many nonprofit institutions fail—or at least do not prosper— because they do not readily understand the nature of their mission as seen through the eyes of their stakeholders.

Third: The Need to Know What Business an Organization Is In

How does a nonprofit organization decide what causal business it is in? The question seems rather silly, doesn't it? A nonprofit organization is in the causal business defined by its mission statement. Its goal, apart from serving those its mission requires it to serve, is to convince individuals to do what's good and right and to get them to follow the organization's agenda, being concerned about the issues the organization talks about and believes in. As part of this goal, the organization typically looks for individuals who are like-minded and who will support it through their donations, purchases, and volunteerism.

Institutions organized this way secure individual support and participation based on issues, societal needs, and the way the organization responds to these needs. It would be accurate to suggest this is a dominant model of nonprofit organizational behavior today.

However, it would be equally accurate to suggest this model does not go far enough for many organizations in their nonprofit marketplace. It represents a way institutions can "market at" people. This is not what donors, volunteers, and customers want or expect from nonprofit organizations they are interested in. Marketing at individuals does not create value for them.

Although many nonprofit organizations talk about being strategic in their actions, using right-sounding management principles, much current practice is at odds with these statements. This operational fact is behind the protests of some powerful and influential donors who have been popularly reported through various fund-raising and business media, as well as of many, many donors who have not been reported on. Though some of these "public" donors have been labeled "virtue capitalists" or "social philanthropists," what the public sees for the most part are two groups of individuals. One group is composed of those who are sufficiently arrogant and hungry enough for publicity to go out and create their own philanthropic vehicles and garner as much attention to themselves as possible. Many of them have been successful in such enterprises, though it remains to be seen what will happen to some of these philanthropic initiatives.

There are others, however, who are unhappy with the current social contract that exists between the nonprofit organizations they support and themselves as stakeholders. The unhappiness of these individuals manifests itself in a number of areas. As noted previously, the principal cause of this unhappiness is the notion that philanthropy consists of supporters handing over their money to a cause and then feeling that their individual duty has been done. "Philanthropy must be more than this," say these stakeholders. Those disagreeing with this old notion of philanthropy feel there must be more than a simple financial transaction; the act should also encompass a loyalty and bond between the individual and the organization based on values and principles important to both parties.

The actions required by organizations to achieve this *loyalty* between parties are sometimes referred to as "relationship marketing," "emotional marketing," or "equity branding" in the business press. The ultimate goal of each strategy, regardless of name, is to create value in the mind of the stakeholder.

How do you define the values that occupy donors and customers? Values are the internal maps that guide a person or company toward those things that are esteemed as having worth or are desirable. For many individuals, their experience with nonprofit organizations often includes being solicited solely on the basis of the organization's need, usually with little attempt by the solicitor or organization to take the individual's interests and prominent beliefs into account. Such corporate actions, designed to create neither loyalty nor good feelings in the hearts and minds of stakeholders, typically lead to some individuals feeling used. However, when an institution decides that donor, customer, and volunteer loyalty is the single most important marketing result they can achieve and are willing to do almost anything to accomplish this, new organizational actions will follow. These actions principally affect

- How an agency organizes itself, its personnel, its physical properties, and its supportive networks to achieve missional goals.
- How an organization conducts its transactions with customers, donors, and volunteers, what it does with stakeholder transaction information, and how this data affects customer service, product and causal innovation.
- How an organization manages and bundles the data that comes from its knowledge and information systems.[4]

Being preoccupied organizationally with value creation in the lives of stakeholders allows nonprofit institutions to become uniquely customer and donor focused while also earning loyalty from their markets. In the book *Emotion Marketing* it is said,

"Customers have a high need to give loyalty—as human beings we inherently need to feel connected with others, to belong. That over 70 percent of Americans question whether there is value in giving loyalty to any company clearly indicates something is missing in what businesses deliver compared to what they promise consumers."[5]

This question cuts both ways. Issues can fade, agency tactics can change, and people do lose interest in organizations over time. Not surprisingly, however, they tend not to lose interest in issues that define their personhood and give them their identity, such as family, religion, hope, morals, dignity, and other values that tend to be relevant to them. Ultimately, these ideas tend to become permanent interests for individuals. To be successful, a nonprofit organization must not only learn to create value around the interests individuals hold dearly but must also be seen by stakeholders as having the ability and wherewithal to solve the societal problems both parties are interested in and meet the need head-on. As this activity becomes intentional at the organizational level, such agency actions provide a volunteer or donor with information that defines the organization, its principles, and the means by which it attempts to succeed in its mission. In addition, it defines those issues that are important to the donor or volunteer.

In today's marketplace an organization must be preoccupied with the values stakeholders hold and the expectations they have for organizational performance. In structuring organizational operations this way, agency leadership must often mandate business, service, and marketing redesigns that best suit the value needs stakeholders exhibit. This is not done as a substitute for good business practices but as components of the agency's management and marketing style. By understanding both the true nature of stakeholder concerns and the core reasons why an institution exists, organizations gain a better chance of procuring a donor, volunteer, or customer's help and commitment over time.

This help in turn, becomes extremely important, because organizational loyalty is simply less important to many consumers today. At a time of many marketplace choices, donors know that should Organization A not do what they want done in an area of concern to them, Organization B is there, as are C and D. If the values of the individual are not mirrored in the actions of the organization, consumers simply leave the relationship. Therefore, it is the individual and not the organization that is dominant in many relationships and that is frequently in charge of deciding the rules of engagement.

Fourth: The Need to Know How to Assess an Organization's Performance

How does a nonprofit organization assess its performance? In one of the preceding examples, the organization's growth and transformation occurred as stakeholders intersected and aligned themselves with it. Each party became aware of the other—their intentions, their values, their lived experiences, and the outcomes they expected as a result of being in a relationship.

Because most nonprofit organizations must by their very nature walk cooperatively with other stakeholder groups to find funding, competent volunteers, or other avenues of support, successful institutions often undertake a series of predetermined actions designed to be cooperative by their very nature. This attempt at mutual cooperation can begin with an organization asking itself and its constituents questions about its performance and direction, and then taking the answers seriously with the goal of taking concerted action together. These include questions such as the following:

Are there better ways to run our organization that will allow us to assist more individuals in our causal work?

What values need to be portrayed by this organization, and will these values change in the next few years?

Is the organization thinking one donor ahead in its marketing and fund-raising strategy and execution?

Without these input and output exchanges, organizations operate on their own and not in alignment with supporting bodies. Operating this way is similar in nature to the popular notion of discussing an agency's "core competencies" but never measuring them to see whether they are indeed competencies.

This effort at aligning one's organization with its stakeholders allows the management team to understand its business within the causal industry it is a part of. Without such an understanding, especially regarding the core values donors, customers, and volunteers hold dear in relationship to an organization, work and effort can be wasted. Worse, donative resources that could be utilized to alleviate the concerns the organization was created for are often not given nor are transactions made, because donors feel placed in unnecessary risk. Opportunities for organizational growth are lost as are opportunities for service.

For some nonprofit organizations, previous successes in service, volunteers, or funding often provide the breeding ground for future failures. Why? Because change, along with the organizational challenges it brings, typically does not arrive on an institution's doorstep in a sequential fashion. Many nonprofit executives were historically taught to take the following steps in the advent of possible change:

1. Gather as much internal and external data as possible by interviewing all possible stakeholders.
2. Develop as many feasible contingency plans as possible.
3. Make your best choice of a plan and implement it immediately, watching closely for signs that you may have made an error; in such a case, begin the process again.

However, these steps may no longer serve as adequate marching orders in the environment many nonprofit organizations operate in today. Instead, executives often face hundreds of factors and scenarios interacting and occurring simultaneously and not sequentially. These executives, who often develop what Pulitzer Prize winner and author James MacGregor Burns calls "the science of muddling through," have few options but to implement a policy of continuously thinking ahead, whether regarding the causal products they hope to use within certain markets, the donors they hope to attract, or the programs they hope to run. In this way, causal industry executives begin to understand the changing patterns of what donors and customers need, want, and are willing to donate to or volunteer for.

There is however, a far more insidious reason why nonprofit organizations are failing. Often focusing so hard on the causal task at hand and all it involves, nonprofit organizations can forget the need to also be equally concerned with the relationships they produce and have with the stakeholders who help ensure the cause's success. As noted, nonprofit organizations are not only in business to care for those in need but to build relational bridges with individuals who need to feel their nonprofit work has meaning as well as purpose, cause, mission, and the ability to give back to society. In the words of a rescue mission board member, "I must believe I can make something happen."[6]

This is a hard balancing act for the nonprofit organization to carry out, because it involves both hard and soft organizational values. In a for-profit company tangible assets determine the company's value and worth. Plants, equipment, buildings, inventory, and profits all can be measured and used to calculate an organization's return on investment. In a nonprofit organization, though, one must not focus on plants, equipment, and profits as much as on service, ideas, and relationships. To be sure, many nonprofit organizations own hard assets and count them as such. However, today's nonprofit organization also competes on the strengths of its relationships, its service abilities, the competency of its people, and the value of these relationships over time.

How do you assess the marketplace impact of issues like these? To do this, nonprofit organizations must first begin to look at services within themselves that create value, move them from the intangible state they may be in (such as the value of a relationship with a donor or the worth of a new program), and begin to create alternatives for the possible outcomes of the relationship or program based on different scenarios and changing assumptions. For example, by asking "How much can we grow this particular donor relationship?" and also asking "How much can they grow this organization?" company officials can begin to reduce these ideas to revenue streams, looking at how much the relationship might cost, how much it might be worth, and when the organization will realize the gain.

Consider an example of this "what-if" analysis involving a doctor who not only donates to a youth organization for at-risk youth but also brings campers to its specialty camps, volunteers for one week a year, and tells her friends about the institution. By looking at all factors involved, an organization can see realistically what could be gained or lost based on the risk associated with negating or building up the future state of this relationship.[7]

The value that resides in many nonprofit organizations occurs within their program departments, their marketing and development units, their ability to create new solutions for the societal problems they face, and the cooperative benefits that come to donors, customers, and volunteers as well as to the organization. Hard assets such as buildings and equipment count less today for many nonprofit organizations. According to Klaus Buechner of Nortel Networks, "one of the largest sources of value is the pool of ideas floating outside the organization. In a world where companies compete on ideas, it's not enough to look in-house; very often, the best minds reside elsewhere."[8]

For many nonprofit organizations today, their marketing unit or department represents the "front lines" of intersection between organizational intentions and donor, customer, and volunteer dreams. This intersection is the subject of Chapter 3.

NOTES

1. *Slywotzky, Adrian J.,* Value Migration, *advance excerpts (Boston: Harvard Business School Press, 1996), p. 2.*
2. *Frumkin, Peter, "A New Era in Giving,"* The National Washington Post Weekly Edition, *October 11, 1999, p. 34.*
3. *Reichheld, Frederick F.,* The Loyalty Effect *(Boston: Harvard Business School Press, 1996), p. 1.*
4. *Adapted from Aurik, Johan C., Gillis J. Jonk, and Robert E. Willen,* Rebuilding the Corporate Genome *(New York: John Wiley & Sons, 2003), pp. 6–52.*
5. *Robinette, Scott and Claire Brand with Vicki Lenz,* Emotion Marketing *(New York: McGraw-Hill, 2001), pp. 10–11.*
6. *From the personal client files of Barry McLeish.*
7. *Richards, Bill, "Intangible Assets Plus Hard Numbers Equal Soft Finance,"* Fast Company, *October 1999, p. 320.*
8. *Ibid., p. 326.*

REFERENCES

Burns, James MacGregor, *Leadership* (New York: Harper Torchbooks, 1978).

CHAPTER 3

The Tip of the Iceberg

Recently I was privileged to speak at a huge marketing and management convention in Orlando. Listening to the many fine speakers comprising the marketing track, I realized anew the performance benchmark of the nonprofit marketing management culture has been raised substantially in recent years. Today it is normative to hear conversations among nonprofit professionals concerning *umbrella* issues in marketing management, including the need for marketing research and the analysis of situational factors an organization finds itself facing, the importance of a SWOT analysis (strengths, weaknesses, opportunities, and threats), and the strength that comes to an organization that strategically positions its communication strategies, name, and brand.

I was caught off guard, however, by the assumptions some marketing track speakers seemed to make. My first surprise came when one speaker spoke of the creation of a marketing "strategy," as though the process was somehow a solitary, lonely pursuit undertaken by individuals with a keen, almost magical, insight into the marketplace. This in fact may be the case for some individuals in whom sheer creativity, ingenuity, and giftedness prevail. For many others, though, strategy creation is a collaborative affair that works in many ways. This collaborative process often starts by reframing old strategic plans and updating them with new practices. Collaboration may also take place between associates at the workplace or in listening to stakeholders in the field. Some gain strategic ideas from agencies that are admired as leaders or innovators in their causal industry as well as from competitors who are making important strides. Seldom, though, is strategy a solitary pursuit.

The second surprise I received at the convention was an assumption some speakers made regarding organizational marketing strategies. For these individuals, the need to have an organization-wide enduring strategy was simply not realistic. They assumed in their lectures that one could not expect nonprofit managers to engage in long-term strategic implementation, diagnosis, and decision-making in the light of marketplace uncertainty (what Peter Vaill calls "permanent white water") and then come up with a working plan that had enduring qualities. There was little need in their minds to have an organizing strategic framework governing an organization's marketing actions. In fact, for most speakers the need to have a dominating, organization-wide strategy was simply missing from their comments.

As I listened further, three underlying philosophies emerged tied to this second assumption. First, it was suggested that the pace of marketplace change no longer allows organizations to have a viable and continuous strategy. An organization-wide marketing strategy was seen as a constraint and a straitjacket placed on managers who often had the need to make immediate causal product decisions. Because economic change, social transformation, and organizational upheaval have all accelerated so much, looking into the future with a strategy that anticipates the impact of these circumstances was simply not possible any more.

The second philosophical point had to do with the nonprofit marketplace being caught up in the change and volatility the rest of our economic culture is caught up in. According to some convention speakers, in circumstances like these the best competitive stance is to strengthen the capabilities of an organization's marketing and leadership team in order to create highly effective product delivery and customer service systems to enhance an organization's reputation. Taking these actions not only allows an organization to point to its quality leadership and efficient operational systems as a positional strategy among other, like-minded organizations; it also leads to a type of competitive advantage in operating against other organizations.

Finally, there seemed near universal agreement among the convention speakers that the presence of the Internet allows organizations to compete on a nearly equal basis. The Internet was viewed as a type of strategy sufficient in and of itself, allowing organizations a chance to display their wares in front of large numbers of individuals who, surfing the Web continuously, were looking for causes to be a part of.

On this day, it seemed to some of the marketing track speakers that the importance of a comprehensive marketing strategy was more readily replaced by the accoutrements of management, leadership, the pace of change, and the Internet. As I thought about what they had said, the speakers seemed to be dealing with only the tip of the marketing iceberg, ignoring three critical issues that skew all marketing discussions today. To find the additional marketing story required an individual to look at the larger, hidden portion underneath the tip of the iceberg.

First: You Must Look Beneath the Tip of the Iceberg to Find Your Stakeholders

How does a nonprofit organization develop a marketing strategy? In theory, it starts by listening to stakeholders of all kinds: donors, lapsed donors, prospects, customers, those who are interested, and those who are not, and finding out what they are saying about the organization.

They are in fact saying something. This is the dawning of the sophisticated nonprofit patron who, with some justification, many authors and consultants are suggesting has arrived. Surveys indicate the typical donor today is better educated than the general U.S. public, with about 54% having completed a four-year degree program or more, whereas the general public is only half as likely to have completed college or gone on to graduate school.[1] Management consultant Peter Drucker calls these men and women, who have a keen sense of their own worth, "knowledge workers." They are not obedient adherents to institutional codes and do not give their loyalty easily. Instead, they tend to bond with individuals and organizations that exhibit similar values and beliefs to their own.

What would a compelling donor experience look like to these men and women? What kind of nonprofit marketing strategy provides such an experience, and what does it look like?

REAL-WORLD EXAMPLES

During the same convention, I returned a call to a director of development with whom I had been playing phone tag. With enormous energy, she announced how disappointed she was with their organization's web site; she wondered whether she should fire the web design team and seemed willing to take what seemed to me a giant strategic leap backward. Citing among other things the cost of maintaining, updating, and running the web site with little immediate return on investment, the director surprised me with her announcement. Over the past five years, the institution had endured sagging fund-raising revenues, some layoffs, and an international office closing. After peaking at $17.1 million in 1999, organization-wide revenues dropped the following year to $16.9 million, then to $16 million in 2001, and were flat the two following years. The director made a telling comment when she said, "I believed our name and reputation would be enough to sustain interest. You can't live in our region without knowing us or hearing about us. I really thought name recognition would do more for us and help overcome our financial slide."*

*From the personal client files of Barry McLeish.

As intimated by its development director, this organization was perhaps a victim of its own arrogance. The director may have also misunderstood what its web site was capable of delivering in this instance. While this story points out the potency of the Internet or its lack of potency, depending on a given Internet strategy, it also makes a comment about the organization's marketing strategy. While it is quite possible the organization was already falling off the radar screen with some members of its target audience before the decision was made to move onto the Web, looking to bandwidth alone to overcome branding and relational marketing limitations among constituents contributed to a series of crucial errors. The organization had stopped listening to its donor base long ago.

How do you create compelling opportunities for donors, customers, and volunteers to be a part of as well as to be involved with the organization? The answers lie beneath the tip of the marketing iceberg and are vast and complex. They go directly to the notion of why nonprofit organizations exist today and why individuals choose to support or make purchases from them. It is here that you find the keys to creating compelling experiences for stakeholders.

Increasing Collaboration through the Power of Value Identification

When an organization routinely listens to its stakeholder base, they are typically confronted with two issues: first, they begin to get a picture of how their constituents describe the causal business the organization is in (sometimes contrasting with the organization's own description) and second, they realize that stakeholder collaboration needs to become a routine part of their corporate culture and is typically missing from it.

These are important issues, because most stakeholders have higher expectations from nonprofit organizations than ever before. Given that some organizations do not respect their supporters intellectually and are not expressively thankful for their contributions as a matter of course, stakeholders can be harder to please and may have a degree of cynicism regarding any institutional relationship. As a consequence, most stakeholders have mental models of what to expect regarding the nonprofit organizations they support. These models help individuals determine what is and what is not appropriate organizational behavior and help govern a person's pattern of response to the institution.

The best nonprofit organizations listen to their stakeholders for clues about these underlying mental models and try to empathize with them and, where incorrect because of a lack of current information, try to change them. From the organization's perspective, the stakeholder's acceptance or rejection of these mental models can serve as an organizing or modifying principle regarding the agency's own strategy development. Depending on the stakeholder's acceptance or rejection of them, these models can have profoundly positive or negative effects on a person's perception of and engagement with an organization.

Listening to stakeholders and attempting to discern their personal models of agency engagement should be at the heart of every marketing strategy. Unfortunately, however, this is one of the most frequently missed first steps in developing a marketing plan.

REAL-WORLD EXAMPLES

A client who works with high school athletes and creates events for them reminds me consistently that they are not in the "events business" per se as much as they are in the fun and memories business. Visiting one of these events involves seeing young men and women having wild fun, forming great friendships, learning life skills taught by knowledgeable staff, and seeing a sense of community beginning to develop—in other words, a total experience. Indelible impressions in the form of memories are created. In looking at the experiences these young people have, as opposed to looking at them merely through the lens of an event, different marketing implications surface immediately. The goal therefore in redefining an organization is to allow it to maximize its marketing potential and focus on the right elements—in the case of these athletic events, skills, friendships, and community—as opposed to elements that would either not sell nor be as appreciated by recipients of the promotional message.

Redefining an organization through institutional listening has a second impact. The level of service and work facing most nonprofit organizations today is simply too large for any one organization to go it alone. There is a need for collaboration. Although collaborative work within nonprofit communities has been going on for decades, the need and ability to strengthen this partnership has never been greater.

The best way to bring about collaboration is to learn by watching how networks in successful nonprofit organizations operate. Collaboration within nonprofit organizations has always been available to those who are interested, whether through volunteerism, boardsmanship, donative support, or helping deliver the causal product directly to those in need. In my mail this week I am presented with the following opportunities:

- To hear lectures from volunteers of a local wildlife group on the feeding habits of winter birds
- To donate food and canned goods to the local food bank
- To send scholarship aid for minority youths going to a sports camp

Unfortunately, many types of opportunities being presented to donors, volunteers, and customers are instigated by most organizations as individual, isolated endeavors. They are not viewed on a continuum of involvement. A person gives a gift and an organization thanks the giver. Someone volunteers and an organization thanks the the volunteer. Unfortunately, many agencies tend to view each instance of stakeholder involvement on a case-by-case basis rather than viewing them all in a synergistic fashion. The real need is for institutions to have a broader focus in their understanding of relationships by redefining their view of potentially collaborative stakeholder activities (e.g., the ones listed) and beginning to understand these individualistic endeavors as values and network opportunities.

What does this mean? Rather than taking a linear approach to individual stakeholders and working with them on a case-by-case basis, some nonprofit organizations are introducing notions of community into their mix and providing for three-way, four-way, or multiple-user opportunities by identifying commonly held values within their networks of supporters, volunteers, and customers. By first classifying and identifying commonly held stakeholder values and then working and reinforcing every stakeholder's activities based on their commonly held beliefs, individuals end up not only interacting with members of the organization itself but with other individuals and their friends, and their friends' friends. The individual no longer works alone in relationship to the nonprofit organization but as part of an extended values community and tapestry network. The common elements of these informal communities—or *tapestry* groups—are the high trust they have in the mission of the organization and the knowledge they commonly share about it, as well as the mutual investments they make to ensure its success.

How do these tapestry groups work themselves out practically? Here are three examples:

1. A rehabilitation doctor volunteers along with other doctors at an organization dedicated to helping a population of young people with a certain illness. Not surprisingly, much of her communication prior to volunteering at the organization's facility for one week was with the sponsoring agency. However, following her time of volunteering, the communication

pattern changed. Not only did the doctor continue to communicate with the sponsoring agency, but her communication pattern changed to one aimed at other doctors who could become potential volunteers to the organization. This type of activity was encouraged by the organization. Today, this group of volunteer doctors discuss each other's volunteer expectations, the procedures they will use at the facility, and the plans they hope to implement on behalf of the young people they serve. They also become involved in other service aspects, recommending the facility to some of their patients and to other doctors who could possibly volunteer. In addition, some of the doctors help fund parts of the agency's operations. These doctors are members of a functioning values network and tapestry community.

2. Businesspeople in a medium-sized community were approached by a nonprofit organization to provide mentoring help as part of the agency's work with juvenile offenders. Starting with only with an initial handful of mentors, the program became so popular and meaningful among the businesspeople that they begin to recruit and train their own members, taking the mentoring program to a different level than the one originally suggested by the nonprofit group. Mutual investment and agreed-on values have led this group to become its own tapestry network.

3. A group of women who are friends came alongside an organization working with families and began to help the organization out by providing many services, from clerical help to office cleaning to family deliveries. Today, this "auxiliary" group numbers about 90, publishes its own newsletter, and helps the nonprofit organization in a dozen different ways. This tapestry community believes in the mission of the nonprofit organization in its entirety and has adopted the agency as its own.

Tapestry or value communities do not come about or form as do networks in the typical technological, Internet sense. Rather, what drives these value communities is the loyalty individuals feel toward their commonly held beliefs, which are typically being mirrored in much of the organization's work. Without such synchronicity, groupings will not form. The internalized values held by the group members become as highly regarded as the organization itself, providing the glue that supports and reinforces the tapestry network; the community increases exponentially as individuals join and add their support, expertise, and help. This renewable, generative source of external support, networking, help, and concern, though diverse and independent, can become as important and powerful as any system an organization would choose to erect formally. The committed individuals, like those in the preceding examples, become both providers to the organization and partners with it.

Why do tapestry communities like these evolve? Simply because values are no longer at the periphery of how individuals choose to involve themselves with nonprofit organizations. With so many good causes to support and be a part of, many donors, customers, and volunteers see nonprofit services and products as commodities, increasingly similar to each other with very little differentiation. Speaking personally, I might say,

> If I am going to volunteer to help an organization, I would prefer to be used in an area that utilizes both my expertise and interest. If I am interested, for example, in creating civic opportunities for older adults and want to use my marketing expertise to help accomplish this, there are dozens of nonprofit organizations to choose from. However, in choosing an outlet for my help, I will only choose an organization that allows me to utilize the personalized criteria I have set up, namely to use my marketing skills on behalf of older adults in the civic arena.

Individuals who are interested in helping nonprofit organizations are often not in a mental, physical, or pragmatic position to see the differences between the organizations that present themselves and are available, and the services they provide. In choosing not only an avenue of service and options that are available, individuals often look at both the espoused values an organization holds and the services they offer on behalf of those values. Choices are then made in order to attain alignment between the values an individual holds, those the organization holds, and the goals each has in applying those values.

In order to survive into the future, many nonprofit organizations will have to look at ways of differentiating themselves from the many similar competitors in the marketplace. One reason for this is that increasingly, most institutions do not have all of the resources they need internally to face the future. This is especially true in discontinuous environments where the organization's past experiences and history do not adequately prepare its leaders for what they are facing. Consequently, by identifying the values an organization exhibits or advocates that set it apart from either competitors or those offering similar causal services and then attracting and encouraging external networks, an agency can begin to develop strategic alliances with groups that will be helpful to it in the future. This becomes an important task as older, competitive positioning models based on differentiating an organization by means of its core strengths or competencies fail to work as well as they once did because of the speed by which competitors mimic the tactics each other displays. No position remains unique forever.

In addition, by moving from a linear strategy of one-on-one collaboration with individuals to a values, network, and tapestry segmentation model in which the values of the organization and those who support it intersect and are shared, formed value communities and tapestry networks allow feedback to take place routinely, allow self-reinforcing behaviors to occur within the communities, and often enable causal growth to take place at rates the organization could not achieve using other marketing, branding, and segmentation models. In addition, they allow agency transaction costs to decrease across many individuals. This fact is supported by the examples previously cited involving doctors, businesspeople, and women, where much of the internal feedback and interaction of these groups is in building up and improving their own services as a whole, as well as those of the organization.

This community and network segmentation model was strongly reinforced to me recently when I talked with a nonprofit group that has a strong social and moral position and is taking this position nationally by creating a new organization. Not surprisingly, the financial supporters the organization is attracting are making their initial determination to support the group first on the values the organization espouses rather than on the core competencies or marketing positions the organization exhibits. It has become strategically imperative to this organization that it align itself with these supporters of a fledgling value network held together by the values its members hold dear.

Moving Priorities from "Organization First" to "Values Network First"

An IBM executive was quoted as saying the organization of the future "must become an archipelago of related activities."[2] This is an apt image for how nonprofit organizations should view their collaborators, all of them distinct in their own right but connected to the organization and each other through agreed-on values and directed communication strategies from the organization, reinforcing and reminding all of the values they share.

Unfortunately, the frequently taught notion in marketing seminars of an organization relating to its stakeholders in a fixed way through communication pieces such as organizational newsletters, frequent direct-mail appeals, and other mass communication devices—all the while trusting that such communication will keep the individuals loyal to the organization—increasingly seems too good to be true in our overcommunicated society. Strongly held, old paradigmatic notions such as believing in never-ending

stakeholder loyalty have simply ceased to be compelling organizational arguments. There must be more for these individuals to hang
onto psychologically in order to create long-term organizational
associations, as the following example suggests.

REAL-WORLD EXAMPLES

Barry and Debby Donor have supported a youth-related
organization for a number of years. Upon closer examination,
it seems the organization and the donor couple are about to part
ways. Why? A number of issues are at stake. The first issue is an
assumption the organization made about the donor couple and
the longevity of their future financial involvement. The second
issue has to do with both the communication pieces being
routinely sent to the couple as well as the invitations both of
them receive to attend events the institution sponsors.

Barry and Debby Donor have little historical continuity or
background with this institution. They received an emotional
direct-mail appeal from it a number of years ago having to do
with orphans. They responded with a check and have slowly
grown their giving over the past 20 months, nurtured almost
exclusively through organizational direct mail and telemarketing. However, the two have become busier pursuing their own
lives and interests and have sensed that the benefits they
receive from their giving to the institution in question are not as
powerful as they might be compared with other opportunities.

If the organization were to talk to Barry and Debby Donor
directly, they might be surprised by the rapidly shifting value
system the couple seems to have. When the couple lapsed in
their giving, the organization responded to the discontinued
relationship by sharply increasing the number of direct-mail
appeals sent to them, trying to revitalize the relationship through
a strong display of emotional giving opportunities. If one could
talk to the organization about the situation, it might seem to
them that this couple has moved from providing loyal support
to the organization to a mind-set that is pushing them away.

Having attracted Barry and Debby Donor to its support base, an organization should first decide what it is going to do to build and maintain a relationship with them. In order to hold onto Barry and Debby and build an alliance with them and around them, the organization's strategy should be to try and maximize the values Barry and Debby represent that are in common with the organization. For many organizations, however, this step represents a tremendous change in strategy and tactics as it moves from thinking of itself first, to thinking of how to maximize others first along with their value networks.

How does an organization maximize a value network? This can be a difficult task, because individual values can change as they move in and out of lifestyle and emotional phases over time. They often migrate quickly from early values formation and organizational membership where optimism exists regarding what the agency will accomplish, to a time of solidity, consensus, and affirmation of certain values with other like-minded individuals, and finally to a time of values embeddedness where certain beliefs become a type of protocol for both individual and organizational modes of action.

When an institution decides to listen to its stakeholders in order to maximize value networks where they exist, it must first be ready to hear things about itself that it may not like. At any given time, most supporters do not support all parts of an organization uniformly and will most likely make it clear what parts of the organization they are going to support and nurture and what parts they are less interested in. This is a natural occurrence. Organizations must find donors and customers who value what the institution is providing overall and where the potentiality of reciprocity exists between supporter and organization.

In the Barry and Debby Donor example (based on a real couple and organization) it became hard for the agency to "risk" listening to too many donors and stakeholders. A much easier option was to continue to mail blanket appeals and hope for the best. Institutions that avoid making hard choices often speak of their strategy as one that is "flexible" with its "options open." However, this lack of leadership and managerial action can also lead to an unfocused strategy that ultimately frustrates an organization, wastes resources, and does not allow itself to maximize the impact of its marketing program or to take into account the values the target market holds in common with the organization.

Unfortunately, an organization can also listen to its stakeholders and not find alignment and congruence between parties in a number of areas. Saying "no" to a group of audience segments that the organization thought had potential as customers and donors is a tough decision for many executives, often accompanied by intense, internal politicking before the audiences are jettisoned for their lack of potential to the organization. Organizations typically hope the situation will rectify itself and a way will be found to appeal to a much larger audience. Hoping the prospective cause will fit with some of the rejected audiences is especially a common occurrence with development directors, who desire to keep all organizational options viable for as long as possible. The situation compounds itself over time, given that while the needs and values of most donors and customers may not change much, their loyalties might.

SECOND: BEWARE THE DANGER OF REPEATING STEPS AND FOLLOWING THEM WITHOUT QUESTION

Many nonprofit organizations have individuals within their donor ranks who support them financially in spite of having little emotional history with the organization. Support still comes to these institutions for many different reasons, though individuals may not have a meaningful relationship or background with an institution.

Donor attachments like these are typically not strategically important to some organizations in the long term, and the feeling is
sometimes equally shared by the donor. It is the here and now that
is often more valuable to both parties. Some donors, filled with "top of
the mind" ideologies and a desire to take advantage of immediate
opportunities, wherever and whomever they come from, embrace
fluid personal values where little may be permanent forever. For such
individuals, life is created on the spot, and it may appear to be a collage
of impressions based on how they feel at the time. Tremendous
flexibility is evidenced by these individuals toward what works,
what is true, what causes they are loyal to, and what they feel is
morally right.

Such individuals can sometimes create some difficulty for
nonprofit strategists. With competition being intense among
many agencies for money, donors, customers, and volunteers,
their survival in the future may not depend solely on their cause or
the causal products they create and use, as much as upon the
models of management and marketing they utilize in the face of
competition. Of necessity, these models have to cope with
profound marketplace ambiguity, uncertainty, and unpredictabil-
ity. A massive shift in the for-profit marketplace has taken place
from supplier-controlled markets to customer-controlled ones;
this shift has also had an indelible impact upon society at large and
the nonprofit world in particular. For example, churches per se
used to have a much larger control of the missionary market than
they have currently. A large church could be a source of both
recruitment and funding for literally dozens of mission agencies.
That supplier-controlled model is changing today as many mission
agencies, operating independently, have moved into the forefront of missions work by securing their financial support primarily from individuals, as well as tailoring their recruitment
strategies away from organizational groupings such as churches.
Many nonprofit organizations, in order to stay competitive and
viable, have learned to step outside outmoded management and

marketing perspectives and reevaluate their modes of operation based on new information and understanding. This has further led to some organizations engaging their key stakeholders in new, innovative ways.

Because the pace of the world has increased, organizations can get trapped in historical ways of operating, paying greater attention to their rules and infrastructure and, in the process, losing the opportunity for real growth. Many of these organizations have some difficulty in surviving today because they do not realize they exist not only to come to the aid of a particular group or population but to provide value and meaning to those who support the institution. "Providing value" is not something institutional leaders think about naturally, nor is it typically considered a necessary part of a marketing or development strategy. However, answering the question of how to provide this value goes directly to the reasons for an organization's existence.

How "value" is transmitted and what it looks like can be answered through a series of *how* and *why* questions:

- Why is the organization operating in this fashion?
- How does the organization grow?
- Why isn't it growing faster?
- Why does it promote its work the way it does?
- How does it introduce new programmatic solutions to its supporters?

Answering these questions begins to force an organization to return to its mission and the way it will be carried out and also leads to "next stage" tactical questions:

- Who is our target customer, donor, or volunteer?
- What parts of our cause are being offered to them for their help?
- In what ways are we asking for their help?

For example, the development team of a nonprofit science museum posed these questions and posited their answers in the following manner regarding a capital campaign being proposed on the museum's behalf:

- Our target donor
  - Individuals who have given over $500 in the last 12 months to the parent organization
  - Individuals who have attended our facility for other reasons and live in the following zip codes
  - Key associational heads of groups in a 50 mile radius including churches, foundations, and associations that have benevolence funds
  - Key individuals who have lapsed in their giving to the museum but gave at the $500 and above level
  - Associates of donors who give over $500 a year to the organization but are not yet donors
- The parts of our cause we are asking help with
  - We are looking to replenish $150,000 from our scholarship fund that is used to get inner city children to the museum free of charge.
- The way we are asking for help.
  - We will create a small dinner event with about 200 individuals in attendance.
  - We will establish an invitation committee of six couples made up of some of our major donors and some key community people.
  - We will invite individuals at the $500 donation range to our event. In the invitation, we will give an in-depth breakdown of what the appeal will be and how scholarship money is currently distributed; we will request their attendance and tell them that at the event we will be asking for their help in the form of a major gift.

- We will stress to all in the printed invitation and at the small dinner event the educational and social benefits to young people of going to the museum.
- We will announce in the print media and at the event that 90% of their gifts will go to the scholarship fund.

Creating Opportunity and Self-Defense

Some nonprofit organizations that fail to ask the foregoing questions would rather imitate the strategic position of their competitors than create a unique position for themselves. Instead of trying to position themselves based on data collected and constituent needs analyzed, these institutions try to adopt the strategic positions other competitors are using and seek to make them their own.

Strategic "winners" generally do not engage in this behavior because it ultimately pits similar causes against each other, competing for marginal gains in their causal market segments. Instead, winners try to create new markets segments where they can initiate their causal concerns and gain a sympathetic ear.

REAL-WORLD EXAMPLES

Consider how a family counseling center in New England used to compete. Its initial response to other competitors was to do nothing. Leadership reasoned there were more than enough clients to go around. As the ability of the organization to grow its customer base diminished, the director of the center, admitting he had been late in seeing the problem, tried to lure customers to his facility through special cost-cutting programs, new four-color brochures, a new curbside sign, and upgrades to his counselor training.

The center's competitors responded in kind. The counseling center leadership responded to these new competitive initiatives by cutting their fees more deeply. Some competitors responded in kind again. The counseling center now had no market position it occupied exclusively. In fact, it began to look exactly like the competition. On the other hand, customers now had a large selection of similar services at a very cheap price. The only way left for the counseling center to gain an advantage it reasoned, was to become smarter than its competitors with better leadership and counselors. It would take a long time though, or so they thought, to establish such a reputation.

Profit margins declined precipitously for the organization. It continued to focus its attention and efforts on protecting and improving its strategic position rather than looking for a way to truly create a source of new advantage.*

*From the personal client files of Barry McLeish.

The counseling center was in an entrenched position dictated by its own strategic choices, complicated by management's inertia and hurt by an outmoded way of competing. It is not hard to imagine oneself in the management meetings of this group, each person anxious about making brash moves in light of the competition for fear that they would destroy the center's market position. What could one do but fight the good fight and be resigned to the situation?

To achieve the type of breakthrough the counseling center required forces an organization to question its accepted practices continuously and to do so in a rigorous fashion. Because of the prevalence of so many competitors in every cause, nonprofit organizations must look at ways to differentiate themselves from others as opposed to merely trying to do a better job in the market segment they have.

Unfortunately, without constantly interacting with an organization's stakeholders, models of who the nonprofit organization thinks it is dominate its strategies. These organizing frameworks, shaping the strategic behavior of the organization, become the narrow gate through which most organizational decisions must pass. Unfortunately, a close adherence to these models allows organizations to become passive by proposing a repetitious series of managerial and psychological "maps" the organization has used before. These maps soon become "sacred cows," dominating organizational thinking and locking out new methodologies or ways of operating.

To develop an accurate marketing strategy, one must first know the prevailing "maps" an organization is comfortable with and begin to question them. Questioning these maps does not mean abandoning them or the ways of operating they embody. However, unless prevalent views are challenged and thought through, the essential elements of strategic innovation—discovering new donors, pioneering new causes, or reengineering an organization's marketing mix—are lost to deeply entrenched ways of operating. Professor Constantinos Markides of the London Business School suggests, "It is not enough to convince people that questioning the status quo is merely important. They must be convinced it is absolutely urgent. To ensure this type of questioning takes place on a continual basis, top management must find ways to make it a top priority."[3]

Author and stewardship consultant Pete Sommer echoes a similar sentiment, noting, "Not only is it important to question organizational 'sacred cows' but a crucial first step in this process is to ensure the organization knows what ministry or social initiative it is in. The reason for wanting to know this is simple. There can be no alignment between the donors, volunteer, or customer and the organization they are engaged in with sacred cows hanging around that are not meaningful to the stakeholder. Organizational refocusing and alignment are at the heart of not only strategic innovation but giving donors and customers a great experience."[4]

THIRD: IS YOUR ORGANIZATIONAL PLANNING AIMED AT CREATING A COMPELLING STAKEHOLDER EXPERIENCE?

Where does planning fit in the discussion of creating a compelling stakeholder experience, especially in the light of nonprofit change and organizational uncertainty? With the decline of some well-established organizations and the difficulty of maintaining a competitive stance for others, interest in organizational planning is reemerging.

Certainly nonprofit planning is different from causal industry to causal industry, and it is different in many respects from the for profit world. During the past several years, few areas of nonprofit business life have attracted as much attention as the process of planning. However, to an outside observer not all nonprofit and for-profit planning seems to play out appropriately in the marketplace. There are certainly well-documented for-profit cases where this has been true. For example, why didn't General Motors see the threat of OPEC, or the Digital Equipment Corporation and IBM foresee the revolution in personal computers? Why were rescue missions so slow in responding to the needs of women and children, or some mission agencies in restructuring how they fund their missionaries?

Most stakeholders are all too aware of the reoccurring cries for help many organizations resort to in order to raise money. Further, they've seen capital campaigns gone awry where the goal was never reached. Was the planning in these instances simply incorrect?

Obviously, something is wrong. No doubt these anomalies remind us that when discussing the issue of planning, it is important to remember three overall classes of information and knowledge available to nonprofit organizations:

- Things an organization knows
- Things the organization doesn't know
- Things the organization doesn't know that it doesn't know

Organizational havoc is often centered on the third point. Intuition would suggest any planning endeavor will encounter difficulty when it has to theorize about its future and is forced to deal with information it does not yet possess and can't deduce about the future. Part of planning's role is to take into account the organization's capacity to either maintain or improve its future performance based on its past experiences—in other words, what it learns, what it hasn't yet learned from these experiences, and how it will utilize the information.

Planning stays within an organization even though people constantly cycle through its leadership and management ranks. To suggest that the role of planning can derive wisdom, sustenance, and benefit from prior individual and agency learning requires organizations to vigorously pursue a constantly enhanced knowledge base from which to plan future courses of action. It is often this same knowledge, accumulated and possessed by the nonprofit organization over time, that allows it to develop new competencies and engage either in transformational (system-wide) or incremental change. In each instance, learning becomes *actionable* and helpful to the organization's planners if there is some sort of integration between the organization's learning pattern and its planning methodology.

Planning for most nonprofit organizations is still carried out in one of four ways:

1. The first is not planning at all but organizational imitation, by which an organization tries to mirror as closely as possible the strategic moves a competitor makes. This is no doubt part of the reason why there are so many similar-looking causes today. Nevertheless, the organization still has a plan of sorts. Organizational listening to its constituents is in this case virtually nonexistent.

2. The second style of planning has to do with organizations that are involved in a stable environment where planning becomes relatively easy. In this milieu, an organizational planning team often develops a forecast of their own future with some certainty based on past experience and can with little effort implement a clear strategy. Though all organizations face some uncertainty as to their futures and hence, no plan is

exact, this kind of planning can often be described as a sufficiently "safe" way for the organization to proceed. In this method there is a tendency to extrapolate actions taken in the past that have been successful and plan for them again in the future as a means of simplifying the planning process. Organizations that feel their environments are stable often find little reason to listen to "outside" stakeholders, preferring instead to trust their own wisdom.

3. The third most popular method by which planning occurs takes into account the presence of uncertainty in an organization's future. In an uncertain environment an organization typically changes how it undertakes setting up its operational and strategic plans. Because of the presence of uncertainty, possible planning alternatives in an organization's future often force its leaders into some sort of scenario planning by which different organization outcomes are envisioned in response to different levels of uncertainty by those in the planning group. Paying close attention to customers, donors, and volunteers often is tremendously helpful to organizations facing environmental turbulence.

4. Scenario planning, along with the other methods mentioned, is not much help in the final model of planning. In the fourth model of planning an organization finds true ambiguity looming in its future. Though this particular planning situation seems likely to be the rarest of the four, one only has to look at some U.S. industries since 9/11 or at post-communist Russia and the industries caught within its borders to see how difficult it has been to survive in a truly ambiguous environment. Planning responses in these situations are usually fundamentally chaotic and not determinative of the future.

In spite of the models listed, most nonprofit organizations operate under some degree of ambiguity at all times. There are always issues looming ahead of an organization that are either unpredictable or unknowable. This becomes especially true if an organization takes listening to stakeholders to heart. When the opinions and values of stakeholders are allowed to become an evolutionary force inside the organization that modifies its behavior, the stakeholders' voice in turn, becomes modified.

Organizational planning at this level can be problematic because of the tendency of most planners toward linear futures and an aversion to the unanticipated. Ron Ward, director of Berea, a large East Coast family and youth facility suggests, "Something new occurs when I listen to my donors. They tell me how to make my organization rich experientially. They help me question the assumptions and beliefs of the organization in a deep way. They question where the organization is going because I am spending their money to get there. Mostly, they want to know if the plans we have made are valid. Do they matter and can they 'win' by following my lead? As a consequence, I have to then figure out how much of my planning is taken for granted and not really tied to either the circumstances or the wishes of my donors. Do I have beliefs that aren't open to question? If I do, I better take a hard look at them before I proceed to make sure they are in keeping with my constituents."[5]

Challenging what an organization holds as sacred about itself, what it believes works in the marketplace, the value that is transferred to stakeholders, and how the organization learns and deals with obsolete ideas must be a continual process. It is often neither easily predictable nor grounded in stability. How to accomplish this is the subject of Chapter 4.

NOTES

1. Campbell Research, DonorSpeak, January 2001.
2. Powell, Walter and Laurel Smith-Doerr, "Networks and Economic Life," in Neil Smelser and Richard Swedberg, eds., The Handbook of Economic Sociology (Princeton: Princeton University Press), p. 381.

3. *Markides, Constantinos C.,* All The Right Moves *(Boston: Harvard Business School Press, 2000) p. 33.*

4. *Sommer, Pete, "Identifying Prospects in Preparation of Personal Solicitation," lecture given at NISET in Madison, Wisconsin, August 1999.*

5. *Ward, Ron, "The Difference Between Theory and Practice," lecture given at CCI's National Convention in Orlando, Florida, November 30, 2000.*

▪ REFERENCES

Vaill, Peter, *Managing as a Performing Art: New Ideas for a World of Chaotic Change.* (San Francisco: Jossey-Bass, 1989).

PeterF. Drucker, *The Age of Discontinuity* (New York: Transaction, 1992).

Bennis, Warren and Philip Slater, *The Temporary Society: What is Happening to Business and Family Life in America Under the Impact of Accelerating Change?* (San Francisco: Jossey-Bass, 1968).

CHAPTER 4

Doing What Matters for Customers, Donors, and Volunteers

hen I was appointed creative director for a large nonprofit organization and then later its development director, I knew one thing for sure: There was no road map to follow. Rather, while working I became aware of having to respond to the myriad of expectations that assaulted me from all directions. They governed my life and came from the president, the president's spouse, some board members, my boss the vice president, and stakeholders from outside the organization. Perhaps the loudest voice of them all was that of my own expectations, thinking that I could fill everyone else's. These issues kept me busy almost all of the time, filling me with anxiety. It was later that I learned these issues had very little to do with what being a development director was all about.

My training had prepared me for being a copywriter, a solicitor, a manager of people, and a nonprofit employee. However, within all of these occupations I had little idea what being a true development professional involved. Few of the seminars I attended had taught me. My advanced education hadn't taught me. I assumed other development directors knew what the profession was all about and what needed to be done with development staff, donors, and the stakeholders I worried about. Even though I had a vague idea about what it meant to fulfill conventional expectations of development work and felt I was doing that part competently and to the best of my ability, I was not yet truly a development officer. I was more like a chameleon; a great deal of my time was spent dealing with demands, requests, and expectations coming from both inside and outside the organization. It was hard saying "no" to these voices, because my assumption was that part of the job of development was living within a paranoid environment and running as fast as I could in response to many, often conflicting requests.

During this time I hoped no one would evaluate my work—or me—too closely. Though our development team income was growing at a significant rate, there was a personal sense of being a fraud to those who supported the work. I didn't like the notion of money being the only indicator of performance; there had to be other social and psychological indicators that would show me a more complete path. I had the good fortune of becoming an expert in personal appeal psychology and consequently taught my staff. They also became experts, and our team's income rose again. My direct-mail programs also became very successful, and agencies and associations asked me to speak to them about what we were doing. In addition, my foundation programs became very large and profitable. Throughout all of this, however, I felt I was selling out, and not only selling out, but selling out as a willing perpetrator. I worked longer hours than others, I did more, and I tried harder. It was not until later that I found out what true development was.

You've no doubt seen the computer screen saver composed of intersecting pipes spilling over everywhere. There may be a pattern that emerges on the screen, but it is one that seems grounded in chaos. With variations in sizes and colors, the pipes change their configuration at a moment's notice. It is easy to forget the pattern.

Many development and marketing directors face similar issues regarding the variance and change in their environments, the nonprofit economy they are a part of, and the wishes of their constituents. The often conflicting wishes of stakeholders and the resulting changes they seek to initiate can be seen as disruptions by development directors and other leaders; consequently, they can become a battleground the directors engage in every day. As a result, many directors wish their marketing and development programs could be standardized and made more predictable. "If only," they joke, "we didn't have to deal with donors and volunteers whose sole function seems to be to confuse issues."

Any organization dealing with donors, volunteers, and customers finds its attempts at variance elimination hindered routinely. Individualized actions by stakeholders are the one issue in institutions that remains irreducible. Unfortunately, many marketing programs assume that individuals can be forced to become like each other and that their response and activity patterns can become truly predictable and the same. Hoping for this predictability by treating audiences as if their response patterns and values were standardized is *the* driving philosophical force behind many nonprofit marketing programs, seminars taught across this country, and consultancy advice. The goal is to portray marketing as having the ability to create standardized, coherent segments of stakeholders who respond uniformly. This view is directly opposed to the reality we find in much of marketing life today, especially after the splintering of mass markets. Authors Don Peppers and Martha Rogers definitively noted this in their book *The One to One Future*, in which they spoke of a future characterized by customized production, individually addressable media, and the need to deal with each individual, one customer at a time.

Not only is a monolithic approach the wrong way to think about some markets, it can also be tremendously inefficient. For example, a development director of a city agency client chose to routinely mail his major donors at the expense of spending significant time with them personally. Having written a letter and sent the direct-mail package, the director may have felt that he had not only communicated with these important individuals but had done so in a timely and efficient manner.

Many other development directors choose a different path, seeking individuals out personally and going through the time-intensive activity of setting up appointments, actually seeing individuals face-to-face, and then following up each visit with further interaction. There is little doubt that one activity is more time-dependent than the other; one activity is harder to manage than the other; and one activity is more stress-related than the other. However, if an organization is interested in maximizing its funding activity with a target market and ultimately creating strong cost-effective efficiencies in its fund-raising, then each individual prospect must be viewed as a market of one, with a tailored request ultimately delivered to each.

Author and lecturer John Kao speaks of "corporate epistemology" (an organization's philosophy of knowledge), clearly differentiating between knowledge required for efficient operations and knowledge required for corporate advancement.[1] What type of information does your organization need today? To fight against the idiosyncrasies many of your donors possess is to fight a losing war. Instead of trying to change their behavior, an organization should look at the beliefs, attitudes, and strengths target audience members exhibit and then focus on these strengths, instead of focusing on what they don't possess. The goal is to obtain the *attention* of individuals according to Thomas Davenport, Director of the Accenture Institute, and John Beck, a Senior Research Fellow, in their book *The Attention Economy*. You achieve this goal not by flooding your organization's stakeholders with e-mails, phone messages, newsletters, or direct-mail pieces they don't want to read; instead, you use the information you have about individuals and build it into your communication activity. By doing this, an organization's leaders can be clearer about what outcomes can be achieved with its constituencies and what cannot.

In 1983, Royal Dutch Shell commissioned a study to look at corporate longevity. The researcher, Arie de Geus, wrote about his findings in a book called *The Living Company* and suggested that most companies are underachievers. In an article explaining his findings he wrote:

> Why do so many companies die young? Mounting evidence suggests that corporations fail because their policies and practices are based too heavily on the thinking and the language of economics. Put another way, companies die because their managers focus exclusively on producing goods and services and forget that the organization is a community of human beings that is in business—any business—to stay alive. Managers concern themselves with land, labor, and capital, and overlook the fact that labor means real people.[2]

Development directors and leaders of nonprofit organizations must learn anew that the way an organization behaves towards its constituents influences its behavior and the outcomes of many of its endeavors. Tactics and strategies, while important, are important only if they also represent the guidance and motivation of stakeholder values. When these individual and agency values are in sync, tremendous energy and synergy between individual and organization is created. As a result, the commitment people have toward the shared enterprise of supporting an organization becomes intensified. Authors James Kouzes and Barry Posner note, "Shared values are the internal compasses that enable people to act independently and interdependently."[3]

How then does an organization begin to prepare itself strategically to truly convey core ideals, principles, and values to stakeholders in order to create a dynamic soul the two parties can share, as well as create consistent innovation, teamwork, and mutual respect the two parties can profit from?

The Background Work in Preparing a Marketing Strategy with Stakeholders in Mind

What does marketing look like today? Has the marketing world changed? Most signs would suggest that "Yes, marketing has changed." Where marketing programs of the past have often seemed closed and rigid, marketing programs today must have an air of flexibility and openness. Where they once seemed to be developed by a few select individuals in a closed room, now marketing programs must respond to values and forces in place. Where marketing directors viewed themselves and their leadership as high atop a pyramid, now astute directors view themselves as part of a circle of activities that surround a customer or donor. Imagine former New York Mayor Rudy Giuliani as a marketing director. After the 9/11 tragedy he brought together many diverse groups into a common agenda while also being able to anticipate where people needed him. He remained calm in the midst of crisis and spoke to many in a way that awakened the values of those around him. Perhaps a successful marketing director acts like this great mayor acted, constantly reaching out to friends, strangers, partners, customers, and donors on behalf of a mission.

Nonprofit organizations involved in large marketing programs often find that upon encountering success, entrenched mind-sets, systems, inertia, and momentum can mitigate against successfully launching new marketing programs. Past successes get in the way of putting customers, donors, and volunteers in the center. Given the increasing number of good choices consumers have today coupled with the sliding degrees of loyalty many organizations find themselves victims of, nonprofit agencies often encounter donors, customers, or volunteers who view their relationship with the nonprofit organization not as a long-term affair but rather like a fishing expedition. If the fishing is good—that is, if donors feel useful, engaged, and value-fulfilled with the organization they have

THE BACKGROUND WORK 81

happened upon—there is a better the chance a particular donor will stay in one place. A nonprofit marketing director must view his or her job as trying to ensure that "the fishing will stay good" through the strengthening of the organization's community of friends, who, like the fisherman, are looking to be engaged in a constant, deep emotional dialog that has a sense of purpose and destiny associated with it.

To create such an environment requires some nonprofit organizations to undergo a tremendous change in how they approach their work. While much is made of listening to stakeholders, it is precisely this task that allows marketing directors and their programs to begin to incorporate closely held stakeholder values they pick up through dialog into their day-to-day activities. Authors Scott Robinette, Claire Brand, and Vicki Lenz in *Emotion Marketing* suggest that successful branding between an organization and its customers has most to do with the emotional dialog that takes place between an organization and its constituents. The more meaningful this dialog becomes, the stronger the linkage between customer and company. More openness toward consumers, more freedom in changing plans to favor new circumstances, and more innovation in conceiving new ways to accomplish marketing tasks—these must become the hallmarks of marketing directors and their programs in the future.

Of necessity, this dialogue starts with the stakeholder.

Starting with the Stakeholder

Professor and CEO Larry Fuhrer has the habit of reminding individuals they have stewardship over just a few things and one of them is time.[4] Fuhrer is the director of Presidential Services, an organization that specializes in serving boards and presidents worldwide in fulfilling their personal and corporate missions. I've had the opportunity to work with Larry on a number of assignments, including running a media-relations center for a large convention of

20,000 collegians. The goal in this assignment was quite simply to make sure the story of the convention was told in the media in positive ways, highlighting both the sponsoring nonprofit organization's ongoing activities and values as well as showcasing the event.

Fuhrer was the consummate one-on-one teacher, starting with the job assignment he gave everyone on the media-relations team. As he talked with individuals about their jobs, he looked in each case for ways to communicate effectively with those he was about to work with for an entire week, often pursuing common ground or similar interests as he talked. Each job was meticulously explained so that the workers knew not only precisely what they had to do but also knew they were not working alone. Any question was encouraged and answered. This was a team event, with each member serving as a backdrop to another, and each participant encouraged and built up. Every individual on the team was important to Fuhrer, and he didn't mind telling them that.

He also backed up his words with actions. If Larry saw a correspondent sitting alone in the media-relations office, he talked to them. If a reporter needed something, Larry found it. His idea of leadership was to lead by example. His idea of marketing the organization to the visiting media was to understand their interests, needs, and concerns and align those needs with individuals and various aspects of the organization being showcased at the convention by the sponsoring organization. By week's end, Larry Fuhrer had talked to most of the media representatives personally, had most likely poured them coffee individually, and knew what stories they needed to file in order to consider their week a success. In all areas he tried to calibrate himself with the interests of the visiting media.

The Role of Strategy

Larry Fuhrer didn't start with tactics in developing his media relations strategy. Rather, he allowed the values and habits of the visiting media representatives to infuse themselves into the very fabric of his media team. His leadership became one of service tied to a core set of values—what the sponsoring organization believed in, what it aspired to be, and where the organization and the values of the reporters connected. Using a sports analogy, he was guided by this playbook.

All of the media team's characteristics—professional competencies, enthusiasm, hard work, emotional energies, and spiritual resources—were marshaled into more than merely providing a good experience to the visiting media. Serving the media and providing them with complete sourcing and satisfaction became a cause that all media team members pursued. This all-consuming vision became both strategy and tactics. Whatever the visiting media needed to accomplish in order to do their jobs and file stories about the event, the media-relations team helped to provide as best it could. Larry Fuhrer led the media-relations team in an expert manner because in his mind, the dialog started with serving the media representatives.

A Reason for Being

"Values-driven leaders articulate the company's 'reason for being.' They convey the company's fundamental aspirations and why they are important." The "reason for being" of the organization sponsoring the media-relations team was evident in how the media team behaved and accomplished its work under Larry Fuhrer. The team's job was to serve the visiting press and put their interests first.

The late director of Spring Hill Camps, Mark Olson, wanted to reinvent the notion of church camp. He wanted to infuse it with an animated environment fueled by intense staff–camper relationships that would generate memories that would not quickly depart from the young people once they left camp. Olson explained, "The notion of most church events or religious camping institutions simply needs to be re-thought. These institutions are often more centered on the message they wish to convey than on the customer who is there and the fun they expect to have while at the facility. 'Fun' is why a kid goes to camp. You must capture it first in your planning. Do that successfully and then you earn the right to convey a message."[5]

Olson was a champion of camping innovation and worked on behalf of the young customers at his camps. Before his untimely death, more than 25,000 young people were attending his camps, with that number growing year by year. With his desire to accomplish large-scale initiatives on behalf of his camper/customers, Olson built his dream by hiring others who agreed with his ideas, agreed to sacrifice like him to reach the goal, and shared his passion for young people. Camping for him was about recreating a model that was old and substituting a new one that was customer driven, fueled by a tremendous commitment to listening to the needs and wants of the customers who came in through the front door. The culture of the organization took this style of listening very seriously and used it to augment its organizational climate, a practice that continues today.

Larry Fuhrer and Mark Olson started with their customers in mind, which became their reason for being, before they put their plans in place.

The Definition of Success

Like many other successful nonprofit directors, Brian Ogne, former chief executive officer of Timber-lee, a facility for young people, was worried about the meaning of success for his organization. It was not enough for him that most individuals inside his organization knew why they were there; they also had to know how they were progressing toward their dreams, corporate goals, and personal goals. According to Ogne, seminars, business consultants, and inspirational leaders can be very gifted in explaining the importance and nature of an organization's vision and how, once embraced and achieved, it then becomes a force for change and improvement in both the organization and society. What they often lack are the steps and building blocks that create a reinforced infrastructure that represents the organization's dreams. "How you define personal and organizational success is how you define the journey you and others are taking together," says Ogne. "Success" is a subject loaded with controversy and not perceived by many to be as easy as merely "knowing what counts and how to count it."[6]

A few years ago, Ogne began a journey that he hoped would demonstrate to his team and key supporters not only a dream for his organization's future, but a dream to build the reinforcing steps to take them there. Facing a highly competitive marketplace, Ogne took some time off to think about how his organization was to compete in the future. Coming back, he began to put together a vision for the future of the agency that would, of necessity, reorganize many divisions, bring in a new chief operating officer, and move Ogne away from the immediate contact he had with the senior managers he loved. In spite of some personal anxiety, he didn't stop there. Ogne put together an activity chart of what needed to happen, an accompanying time line for when it needed to happen, and simultaneously began a search for a chief operating officer. During this time many, many meetings occurred between him and his staff, with dozens of questions emerging that required solutions.

Ogne did not lose sight of his goals and vision. He constantly went back to his vision for the future as it was evidenced in his time line and plan. Routinely charting progress with his staff and updating organizational issues when necessary, Ogne did not allow his team to lose sight of the goal. With his commitment being tested frequently, he nevertheless constantly moved over his charted stepping stones of progress toward what he felt was right for the future. The new chief operations officer was hired according to his plan; since then, new tests, unanticipated issues, and organizational matters have arisen. Nevertheless, the success–driven goal of reorganizing the organization for the future prevailed, as did the measures taken to achieve that goal.

IMPLEMENTATION AT ALL LEVELS

Brian Ogne felt his job was to articulate a future for the organization that could be realized, and then to define this future as a series of steps to be taken by the institution to achieve it. He defined this "future" in terms of the values Ogne felt his organization would have to mirror in order to achieve the vision. In the process of working toward this future state, all levels of the organization were affected.

How does a nonprofit leader make sure his or her behavior and vision for the future affect all levels of the organization in a way that brings trust into the process? The first step is letting everyone see and feel what you as a leader are doing and what you believe in. Then you must live out these beliefs every day in the way you execute your office. Ogne demonstrated his beliefs by letting all employees have a say in the future of the organization. In this process, his values were demonstrated, and they in turn, reinforced his behavior as chief executive officer.

Through frequent meetings and an open-door policy, his employees could meet to discuss the implications of proposed change for the future. There was tremendous emphasis on face-to-face communication. Those that chose to not get involved in these discussions learned of them through company interoffice communiqués. The emphasis, however, was on people staying in touch with each other and the events as they unfolded. The community of office workers was engaged through meetings, forums, executive briefing sessions, and individuals who demonstrated strong values-driven leadership. Ogne and his managers reached out to employees, board members, and other partners to help them feel they were a part of something that was important, vital, and exciting. As Paul Judge, a columnist for *Fast Company* notes, "Good communities are not built on monologues. Provocateurs try to create a feeling that no walls separate the company from the outside world. The goal is constant interaction—with customers and prospects, with other businesses, and with suppliers and regulators."[7]

Successful change cannot happen with others without believing it is possible and without enough trust in the process to allow it to happen. Trust becomes the glue that reinforces the strength of relationships. Without trust, there is little chance not only to bring stakeholders together, but to set and achieve a common goal and instill a sense of belonging in the lives of those involved in the process. Belonging then allows better communication to take place so that all are welcome, from those who are core to the process to those who choose to stay on the periphery.

Independent and Interdependent

It is not unusual for a nonprofit director to attend a fund-raising conference or workshop and, once there, to be regaled by stories of how donors, volunteers, or customers have "gotten in the way" of a good program or event. While it may not be unusual for this type of conversation to occur, what is more unfortunate is that many directors have not kept pace with the reality of today's marketplace. The new economy nonprofit organizations find themselves in is all about the exchange of relationships. Donors, customers, and volunteers must "own" a different place in organizations today. Many of these individuals want a say in how organizations are run or financed. Some act more like shareholders or owners than disinterested parties. When asked how he keeps his labor costs so low, Ron Ward, executive director of Berea noted, "We make extensive use of volunteers who have a personal stake in how our operations run. For example, when something goes down or fails mechanically, it is not unusual for volunteers to completely deal with the issue and resolve it before I hear about it or have to deal with it. These men and women, 'run the place' in both the psychological and the pragmatic sense through their volunteerism and donations and enjoy a huge measure of personal ownership."[8]

However, for a nonprofit organization to competently appeal to an external group of stakeholders, as illustrated in the preceding example, there first must be a sense of belonging and continuity among the internal employees of the organization. When achieved, this sense of continuous belonging can most often be seen in the commitment expressed by employees to the organization and the practices the organization builds into the relationship with its employees. For many organizations this reciprocity is not easily achieved. There has been a strong emphasis in conferences and books of the past several years on specialization of tasks within nonprofit organizations. It has become easy for organizations to treat their employees as disaggregate components, with little bother or thought by management of how to put individuals or departments together to better accomplish corporate tasks. While most nonprofit organizations readily understand how their component parts function, many agencies do not understand equally as well the interrelationship between these component parts and the way to marshal them to work and accomplish tasks jointly. Thousands of nonprofit organizations have succeeded wonderfully in building independent departments and specialized operations. Now the task for many of them is to figure out how to work interdependently.

Allowing groupings or units of employees both to exhibit independence in practice and to function as part of a larger, interdependent network introduces stress and tension into most organizational communities. Quite frankly, many nonprofit organizations would rather not function this way. Coming out of highly directive organizations or command-and-control cultures as many nonprofit organizations do, it is much easier for these groups to expect that a "leader" will come up with strategies and that those serving under this individual will then implement these strategies. For these organizations, reinventing how they operate is often crucial.

Trust across different employee networks also needs to be cultivated. Once achieved, though, these trust networks allow processes to function interdependently while operating independently, allowing information and ideas to move across departmental boundaries and become a type of glue that can bind a nonprofit organization together.

How does an organization achieve a culture that is both independent and interdependent? This is not a natural choice for some agencies. Unfortunately, many of these institutions must accomplish cultural change by forcing departments and individuals with different functional and interpersonal backgrounds to work together in common tasks under time and performance pressures. Though "forcing" sounds harsh, in some nonprofit organizations it is not normative within their operational cultures to allow or expect individuals to understand what other employees can contribute departmentally and why their contribution is so important. If management does not allow such cross-pollination to occur internally, literally thousands of nonprofit agencies simply will not view the benefit and synergy of combined operations and their employees as seriously as they need to.

For example, a classic type of organizational mistrust can often be found between nonprofit accounting and program teams. Each team typically starts with a different perspective on what is needed in the marketplace, and each speaks from a different cultural viewpoint, one concerned with profit and loss and the other concerned with providing customers with what they want or need. Both concerns are obviously needed and important in the life of an organization. In the course of their work, the majority of nonprofit institutions have found that what is appreciated by donors and customers is also good for their causal work. Vice versa, the majority of decisions organizations make on behalf of those they are serving are usually applauded by those funding the work. Each viewpoint is needed. Holding fast to the meta-values that hold the institution together, these organizational units not only *can* work together successfully but *must* work together. To fail to do so relegates each to a cheerleading and advocacy function within the nonprofit agency, each unit trying to get its own program instituted instead of each unit contributing a unique capability. However, for this unique departmental partnership to occur, the individual units first must be given a chance to do this and a reason for doing it.

Unfortunately, these organizational issues are seldom dealt with at seminars or by consultants. In years of development conferences, how many seminars have been given on how accountants and program staff should work together? This is unfortunate, because intense interaction between teams over time not only allows for diverse views to come forward, but also typically allows for a higher quality of recommendations and decision-making to emerge. However, the failure to take other departments, their opinions, and their reactions seriously into account ultimately affects not only the internal staff, but stakeholders who are outside the organization. What happens or doesn't happen inside an organization has a direct bearing on donors, volunteers, and customers in terms of organizations listening—or not—to their opinions, including them in the decision-making process, and developing interdependent action plans. Not looking inside and outside an organization for synergy is perhaps the most serious cultural and tactical error some nonprofit organizations make.

Achieving this relationship and the commensurate commitments internally can be tricky. A large number of nonprofit organizations outsource certain business practices and activities and well employ individuals who work from their homes, often online. Organizations finding themselves in these situations often seem to have a different type of commitment to those who work away from the organizational site and vice versa. It is not unusual for the work to ultimately become centered on contractual expectations as opposed to mutual loyalties. To ignore these relationships can have the same detrimental effect as some of our previously cited examples.

Building a New Box

A female executive I will call Barbara heads up an organization facing a unique challenge. Though the organization is characterized by values of excellence and innovation, her nonprofit agency is in trouble. In spite of the fact that she and her team struggle constantly not only to meet but to exceed customer and donor expectations, the organization has been in a financial slump for months and now it's as if the entire team is desperately looking for ways to overcome the organization's market position as well as enhance its competitiveness. Surprisingly, Barbara and her team seem to know the reason why their cause is in financial straits. The reason is in fact either good or bad news, depending on one's relationship to the organization. "I never expected to see or experience this," says Barbara, "and in fact, I really know of no organizational or marketing management models to help me anticipate and decide what I need to do next as Director."[9]

Based on extensive stakeholder listening done by the team as well as other market research studies they have paid for, the problem Barbara and her team face is that they are perceived organizationally to be "winning" in their state-wide advocacy work. During the past five years, the agency's leaders have not only achieved many of their service projections but have gone on and set higher standards of work in their casual field. As a team, they have been flooded with accolades from the national association they are a part of, have received many congratulations from active donors and supportive members, and have been noted in the media for the way they have approached their service issues.

However, after the high points of their success occurred, the accolades began to recede as did support. Barbara and her team had succeeded in laying out a vision that had captivated donors, consumers, and legislators, many of whom also supported Barbara's nonprofit organization. Their support made sense; the agency seemed to be worthy of their interest. These individuals therefore showered the organization with philanthropic gifts, psychological support, and some volunteered to help.

That was yesterday. Today, tough times have arrived. Many donors—a number of them in the "major donor" category—have reallocated the bulk of their gifts to other causes, feeling both that they have already "won" in this causal arena and that their support role is no longer urgently needed within Barbara's agency. Further, competitors have also arisen that have not only mirrored Barbara and her team's advocacy approach but have also mirrored their causal agenda and legislative tactics, siphoning off some of the organization's support. Further complicating matters, untrue accusations leveled at Barbara and her team by some competitors have caused some public-relations problems. At the time, these incidents seemed like small problems to Barbara. Further, some key legislative stakeholders began to grumble because of the accusations being leveled at the organization, as did some of Barbara's board of directors. Growth began to stall due to a slump in donations. Some employee positions were laid off and not filled again. On top of all of this was the perception held by many supporters that Barbara and her team had "won" as much as they could in their work.

A situation that would have thrown many executives into a downward spiral did not throw Barbara. Dealing with the world in the way it was and not the way she wished it would be, Barbara and her team began pulling away from programs that had marginal success in the past, strengthening others that were already strong, and viewing the entire situation as a corporate learning experience. Past and present donors, customers, and other key stakeholders were kept informed and listened to, again and again.

The goal was simple: Barbara and her team had to make sure they had the issues right. They also had to set a direction the organization's supportive constituents could agree with, and in the process, had to work with the entire team to get everyone pulling in the same direction.

Barbara and her team also began to think the unthinkable. Traditional ways of handling the issues they faced no longer worked. "It was clear a large segment of our market felt that we had done a great job in some areas, and many of them emotionally had declared 'victory' in their personal lives and were ready to move on. They were not interested in a long-term financial commitment to a cause they felt was under control. The urgency was gone. It was important for us to accept where this industry was in relationship to our cause, and it was very important for us to think in terms of survival or closing shop. The issues got clear very quickly."[10]

Barbara and her team looked very hard at their own competencies, what their supporters would and would not support, and decided on a plan to accomplish two agendas. The first was to maximize their commitment to the market they were in, in a cost-effective way to ensure that all of the work they had put into it would not splinter apart. Second, they decided to look at entering a new market.

According to Barbara, "We knew there was part of the market that had not benefited from what we could accomplish organizationally, so we looked hard at our core organizational competencies, talked to our donors about entering a new market, and then listened to what they had to say. At this stage, it would have been suicide not to have listened to them."[11] As a result Barbara and her team advanced into a new market slowly but purposefully, beginning to do great work there while continuing to work in a reduced way in their original causal market.

When donors and stakeholders began to move to other nonprofit organizations and away from hers, Barbara and her team did not close the doors to their agency. Instead, they first stayed as closely related as possible to their donors. These were donors who had once expressed interest in their cause and hoped that the organization might come back and support a related endeavor. Barbara and her organization did not know what the future held and chose not to burn bridges organizationally. In addition, a lot of corporate listening occurred on the part of Barbara's team, as did ultimately a change in some of their service focus. This would not have occurred unless Barbara and her team had first decided to go the course.

THE NEXT STEPS

The people talked about in this chapter—Mark Olson, Brian Ogne, Larry Fuhrer, Ron Ward, and Barbara—had to develop an understanding about how to face the issues in front of them organizationally and, in some cases, had to think and act in ways that were initially unfamiliar to them in order to accomplish their mission. In the case of Brian Ogne and Barbara, the way issues were "fixed" required transformation in the cultures they were a part of. Larry Fuhrer also dealt with organizational culture, but in his case, the challenge was to create a dynamic culture of performance and accountability to achieve the organization's stated goals.

These individuals sought to manage the situation they found themselves in and determined not to let the situation manage them. They all determined the results they needed to achieve and strove to reach them. In addition, they all had to think about how their actions were going to be accountable. To accomplish these end results ultimately required having a firm grasp on the reality of each situation, a sense of how to solve the problems, and a relentless drive to reach the solutions.

These actions then became the tactics that these leaders employed in dealing with the experiences they encountered and formed the beliefs they superimposed on their situations. This created a path in their minds to clearly defined end results.

Having a clearly defined path is also important in developing an agency's strategy, whether one is talking about a marketing strategy or an organizational strategy. Developing this path and the resulting mind-set is the subject of Chapter 5.

▓ NOTES

1. *Kao, John,* Jamming *(New York: HarperBusiness, 1996), p. 9.*
2. *de Geus, Arie, "The Living Company," in* Harvard Business Review, *March/ April 1997, p. 52.*
3. *Kouzes, James M., and Barry Z. Posner,* Credibility— How Leaders Gain and Lose It, Why People Demand It *(San Francisco: Jossey-Bass Publishers, 1993), pp. 121–122.*
4. *Berry, Leonard L.,* Discovering the Soul of Service *(New York: The Free Press, 1999), p. 40.*
5. *Personal conversation with the author, June 1999.*
6. *Personal conversation with the author, December 10, 2001.*
7. *Judge, Paul C., "Provocation 101,"* Fast Company, *January 2002, p. 111.*
8. *From the personal client files of Barry McLeish.*
9. *From the personal client files of Barry McLeish; the organization's name and that of the director have been masked for reasons of confidentiality.*
10. *Ibid.*
11. *Ibid.*

▓ REFERENCES

Davenport, Thomas H. and John C. Beck, *The Attention Economy* (Boston: Harvard Business School Press, 2001).

de Geus, Arie, *The Living Company: Habits for Survival in a Turbulent Business Environment* (Boston: Harvard Business School Press, 1997).

Peppers, Don, and Martha Rogers, Ph.D., *The One to One Future* (New York: Currency Doubleday, 1993).

Robinette, Scott, Claire Brand, and Vicki Lenz, *Emotion Marketing* (New York: McGraw-Hill, 2001).

CHAPTER 5

The Mind of the Nonprofit Strategist

Every day of their managerial lives, many nonprofit leaders must make painful allocation decisions as they confront the few resources they have available to them to accomplish their core mission and tasks. Although managers typically want to build more effective organizations that advance and show progress toward achieving their goals, this nagging issue nevertheless serves as an institutional obstacle, blocking all a leadership team hopes to accomplish. In addition to affecting the employees in a negative manner, the lack of organizational resources can have a negative effect upon those outside the organization. Whether one speaks with donors, customers, or volunteers, partnering with an organization that is "just scrimping by" can affect their loyalty toward the institution and the satisfaction they feel in being involved. Almost all stakeholders, when given the choice, want to be a part of an organization that is doing more than "just making it."

Of course, the simplest organizational response to a lack of resources is to find ways to supply the institution with more resources. In fact, the vast majority of successful nonprofit organizations exert great amounts of energy doing exactly this. Unfortunately, not all nonprofit leaders are able to secure the financial futures of their agencies. They may lack the desire, wherewithal, or capacity to do so. Others take a different tack. Instead of searching for ways to add resources to their institution, some nonprofit leaders are doing just the opposite. These men and women are rigorously cutting costs, downsizing staff at all levels, and "getting lean and mean" to find the needed resources within their organization to continue operating. Often made reflexively and in isolation from other operational and customer concerns and possible strategic opportunities, such managerial choices, taken to their natural conclusion over time, often have deleterious effects upon an organization. Instead of growing both the resource base of an institution and transferring new and existing resources into arenas that might yield a higher value in their usage, some managers are choosing to "destroy the current organization in order to save it for the future." Even though this is an approach some managers choose, it has the effect of simultaneously gutting agencies of their key systems and people, often resulting in highly inefficient infrastructures and services that become skeletal in nature. In addition, management initiatives like this one can demoralize an organization's entire stakeholder base, starting with employees and rippling outward to its donors, volunteers, and customers.

A Different Way of Operating

Why has there been this significant pulling back from investing in organizational and infrastructure systems on the part of some nonprofit leaders? The most consistent responses from executives when asked this question are (1) the emotional difficulty they have in justifying the cost of a strong, sustainable infrastructure support system in the light of the massive need they are serving (to say nothing about the difficulty of raising this type of money) and (2) the problems in assessing real-time financial and/or program benefits from their current infrastructure operations. Unfortunately, some nonprofit managers have not seen how well-thought-out infrastructure services and systems can be designed to be of paramount strategic importance in achieving organizational success. Nor have they experienced how an effectively created infrastructure aids in realizing the kind of stakeholder collaboration many agencies are trying to achieve today.

To achieve sustainable collaborative success between an organization's stakeholders and its infrastructure—or "back room" functions—three critical problems must be understood and addressed before a framework for a different way of operating can be developed.

First: The Stakeholder Problem

Attempting to get the necessary funding for infrastructure support has not only proved difficult for many nonprofit managers, but in some cases it has been found unrewarding. As seen through the eyes of donors, customers, and volunteers, the perceived value return of helping to fund such a project and the desired impact it is to make on an organization (and its supporters) is often seen as suspect because of half-hearted institutional commitments to its success along with ever-present poor implementation practices.

A key issue in undertaking ventures like this may have to do with the fact that many proposed infrastructure changes do not explicitly address at their creation the potential they have in creating value for customers, donors, and volunteers. For example, experience suggests that dozens of capital campaign building projects focus almost entirely on the agency's desire for a new structure and do not take into account how the project will result in the delivery of better services to donors or customers whom the organization might want to keep as supporters or those it needs to attract in the future. Agencies building new structures tend to simply assume the new plant will accomplish this, but they seldom discuss the issue overtly in the planning process, nor do they have any type of benchmark or goal for the building process. A current example is that of a client that wants to build a new headquarters. At the six-month stage in the planning process, more discussions have occurred about the need for whiteboards in every office cubicle than the impact the new building may have in serving stakeholders more efficiently.

Unfortunately, the list of possible needs an agency may have in the initial planning stage that shows little regard for stakeholder concerns and values doesn't stop with new building projects. Virtually every nonprofit institution at one time or another wants to replace the phone system, update computer software and hardware, refurbish the mailroom, and so on. The list is often justifiably long. However, many donors, customers, and volunteers, hearing of these needs for the first time, are often not convinced the initiatives are worth the effort and may doubt that the changes will significantly improve operations within an organization. Agencies typically forget that stakeholders want to know, "What is in the improved operation or new building plan that will benefit me personally or those the institution serves?"

In addition, some agency leaders are guilty of assuming that infrastructure changes can do more for an institution than is actually possible. Consider the all too frequently told horror stories about the inadequacies of company-wide computer system update initiatives. Too often after infrastructure changes have been implemented, mistrust and adversarial relationships are created between the agency and its stakeholder partners when promised stakeholder benefits are not realized. For example, in one company a client promised stakeholders on line registration for its programs. The day registration opened, the system crashed, bringing not only angry complaints but a lingering doubt on the part of stakeholders as to whether the organization could deliver what it promised. Obviously, situations like these become immense organizational and public relations problems that can take years to overcome in the minds of some donors and customers.

Infrastructure changes must begin with a clarity of purpose distilled in the question, "Why are we doing this?" The nonprofit management team must create within its stakeholders a degree of confidence that the benefits about to be created through the organizational changes transcend the costs incurred and, additionally, increase the value level of the agency to the stakeholder.

Second: The Planning Problem

The second challenge facing infrastructure management has to do with the planning of organizational change. Unfortunately, some infrastructure changes have more to do with an executive's discontent with his or her current operations than with a clear estimation of the potential need, the benefits that will be gained by changing the situation, and the solution that is required to achieve these benefits. In a negative example where this kind of planning was not done, a client built an expensive boardroom for $125,000. According to the staff person in charge of this boardroom, since its completion two years ago, the room had been used an average of 26 days per year. Unfortunately, many stakeholders questioned the decision to build the boardroom and the allocation of hard-to-come-by funds for that purpose.

The relatively simple though extensive work needed to plan for a beneficial future course of action was not done by the executive in charge in this case, and it is often not done by executives when personal preferences are in play. In the case of the boardroom, the chief executive officer felt she needed a place for high-level meetings. What the organization got instead was an expensive luxury that is now both underutilized and not very helpful organizationally. The pertinent information was not looked at before the project was begun, and the resulting decision to build was not as helpful as was promised and expected. Consequently, the rewards for this project were short term in nature and benefited only a few individuals.

Ideally, infrastructure changes need to increase the service potential or value realized by those who collaborate, support, or work with an institution, thereby creating systems responsive to the needs of the institution itself and those who are its stakeholders. In the case of the boardroom, neither group was served well. Though there are planning tools available to agencies to help eliminate this type of mistake, individuals in organizations typically plan in isolation, not focusing on the larger environments they are a part of. Nor do they look at the benefits that come from involving multiple departments and different groups of stakeholders in a project. Instead, agency heads often consider involving "outsiders" as an obstacle to completing a project.

Taking others into account in the planning process yields real benefits to an organization. A client rebuilt the agency's mailroom to accommodate organizational growth. As soon as the project was given the "go" by management, the mailroom supervisor and the development officer talked in advance to customers and donors outside the organization as well as department heads and staff inside the organization to determine how to better to serve both groups of customers. Informed by focused, intelligent information, the mailroom redesign helped create a competitive advantage for the organization through the leadership's willingness to design systems and services based on the concerns and needs of others. Gains were realized in all areas of service.

Third: The Focus Problem

The third challenge has to do with organizational focus. This can be a "good news/bad news" issue. Many leading nonprofit agencies have realized significant financial benefit during the past several years by integrating internal, disparate departmental services for accounting and cost reasons. For example, one organization merged receipting with accounting. The move seemed simple enough and resulted in a cost savings by utilizing accounting clerks who had time on their hands to do the receipting as well. The organization benefited from these internal moves financially.

STEPS TO SUCCESS 103

What they hadn't factored in or realized was the steady stream of *informal communication* that went on previously between the receipting department and the agency's supporters. When personal, handwritten notes of greetings and thanks stopped appearing on sticky notes attached to the receipts and thank-you letters going to the agency's donors, and when phone calls to the department were answered only perfunctorily and as factually as possible, the chief executive officer of the organization started getting his own calls from donors. The departmental moves had made sense internally, but they did not provide significant external value to the organization's stakeholders through improved services. The organizational goal was "cost savings," not collaborative commerce. Being focused exclusively on the bottom line like this while at the same time obtaining significant infrastructure performance improvements in the eyes of stakeholders is almost impossible unless the organization focuses on expanded levels of service in all directions. Without this focus, what was touted as a strategic solution to an existing problem frequently pays off internally but may be viewed by stakeholders as a failure.

The focus behind infrastructure changes must be one in which all players are effectively served, not just adjacent internal departments. All enterprises in an organization's network—internal and external—must be included in an organization's infrastructure strategy.

STEPS TO SUCCESS

Is there a better way to think about and plan for an organization's future success? The answer is "yes!" There is also some urgency to this need. The combined issues of finding more operational resources to use, lengthening the life cycle of stakeholders, and creating future options for nonprofit economies has never been more important to an organization's survival than now. With so many social issues appearing to be both unsolvable in the near future and systemically intertwined with each other, organizational leaders must begin thinking beyond their own tenures to ensure the survival of their institutions and the work they do. Not only is there a future need for the service of many nonprofit agencies, but adopting a long view managerially can lead an organization away from the negative option of digging the hole it finds itself in any deeper through the destruction of its infrastructure.

However, for an agency to move away from a "lack of resources" mentality and culture—often expressed institutionally and culturally as having little concern as to the length of time supportive stakeholders are involved—to a new way of operating, a decision must first be made. Is the organization willing to move philosophically and culturally from old notions of how to relate to its constituencies to new organizational and marketing models of stakeholder value creation and interdependence? This cultural and philosophical shift is typically accomplished only when an organization's leadership team adopts a different view of how the agency should operate. Shifting an agency's thinking as well as its operating business culture—especially when it comes to moving from institutional and historical views that have suggested audiences are to be treated as little more than passive observers—may not come easily for some organizations.

In fact, the notion of viewing stakeholders as a group to be admired and worked with flies in the face of much of the popular logic driving many of today's nonprofit marketing cultures, seminars, consultants, and authors of books. Often, the philosophical drivers behind these institutions, events, and publications aim to enhance an organization's efficiency within its existing programs before anything else is done. This logic is fine as far as it goes. All programs and organizations can and need to be improved. However, the logic does not go far enough.

A new model with different thinking—other than that of delivering a more efficient operating environment—needs to be considered. The stage for this suggestion is set by Max DePree, chairman emeritus of Herman Miller, Inc., who argued in *Leadership Is an Art* that business leaders must treat their top employees as volunteers. Can this notion be expanded to all stakeholders? The following example demonstrates the need for this view.

REAL-WORLD EXAMPLES

A nonprofit organization I worked with had a highly aggressive direct-mail program, with some audience segments receiving as many as 22 appeals per year. In addition, receipt mail was sent whenever a financial gift was given. The direct-mail program ran like a finely tuned machine and dealt with its intended audiences solely through marketplace rules—that is, income-to-expense rules. As long as the direct-mail program raised money with appropriate income-to-expense ratios, there was little need (according to management) to interfere with its efficient operation.

When I took on a market research project on behalf of the institution (one that was not related to the direct-mail operation), my conversations with donors were dominated frequently by their complaints and threats to leave the organization, both psychologically and financially, if the direct-mail engine aimed at them was not turned off. Many of the donors simply felt abused, mistreated, and not listened to, in spite of their complaint calls and letters to the parent organization. When I presented these findings, the organization refused to listen or to do anything about the sizeable number of complaints. Instead, it continued to adopt a posture that left little choice but to get every dollar from the increasingly unhappy public as efficiently as possible. The organization simply felt that it could not turn off its direct-mail machine and remain competitive. Not surprisingly, a number of employees had given themselves "no mail" codes so as not to be buried under the avalanche of mail being sent out.

Rather than trying to create value for their stakeholders through their direct-mail solicitations, this organization was more interested in appropriating value from individuals while maintaining an efficient operation. It viewed donors in economic terms through a short-term lens. Building an efficient direct-mail system became more important to the organization than building people; the relationship with the donative public was viewed in purely economic and market terms. As long as there were sufficient numbers of individuals to prospect via direct mail, the model would not change.

Any organization continuing along this short-sighted road will see its focus naturally and increasingly becoming more self-centered. As long as an institution has the ultimate goal of solely creating value for itself—as opposed to mutual or joint value creation with its stakeholders—there is little chance to create truly a strong, interdependent organization. Professors Sumantra Ghoshal, Christopher Bartlett, and Peter Moran refer to this notion of mutual interdependence as "building shared destiny relationships."[1] The phrase suggests organizations should strive to create value internally and externally with significant effort spent on expropriating as much value as possible, not solely for reasons of altruism but because it makes business sense to empower and energize stakeholders on behalf of the organization.

How does an organization begin to operationalize this sort of strategy? Are "shared destiny relationships" simply a nice perspective, or can they actually be fleshed out using a series of operational tactics?

At its essence, creating a shared destiny relationship with a donor, customer, or volunteer speaks to how an organization chooses to do business with an individual and what it chooses to do with stakeholder information. Most readers are familiar with the "information glut" bombarding consumers monthly, daily, and hourly. The statistics are staggering: "The U.S. Postal Service delivered over 230 billion pieces of mail last year, and approximately 1 billion e-mails were sent over the Internet on an average day."[2] Depending on the research an individual reads, somewhere between 54 to 93 e-mails are sent to the average e-mail user weekly in this nation.[3]

In light of this "communication din," how do organizations and stakeholders receive and reciprocate with those they communicates with? Seth Godin, a former Yahoo executive, suggests in his book *Permission Marketing* that individuals like to be marketed to in categories they find appealing and acceptable. They simply do not want to deal with unnecessary information and advertisements. In fact, it is increasingly becoming normal for stakeholders to listen only to organizations that use an individual's personal information wisely. The correct use of this information easily becomes an asset to an organization, especially information that allows an agency to know why an individual supports its cause or buys its products.

"Useful information" can be a two-way street. Highly usable organizational information is important to stakeholders, allowing consumers of all stripes to be able to hear, see, and access helpful facts about the organizations they are interested in. Institutions, as well as donors, volunteers, and customers who entrust personal or corporate information to each other, feel they are realizing value in the exchange process when the information is used in appropriate ways.

What is an "appropriate way?" Two illustrations from clients superbly demonstrate how this can happen in the lives of both stakeholders and institutions. In a recent example, a donor of a client referenced a "P.S." in a letter he had received more than six months earlier from the chief executive officer suggesting the organization in question had a desire to help a particular group of young people but lacked the resources and wherewithal to do so. Upon seeing the executive officer socially at a public event, the donor casually asked the director if the need was still apparent. Hearing that it was, the donor mentioned some property that might prove helpful in solving the need and suggested he and his wife would like to buy the land for the organization. The purchase of the 238 acres by the donor couple for the organization's new program occurred because in the postscript of a personal letter, the director had given the couple some information useful to them.

In another example, a field representative for a client remembered that in their conversation a particular volunteer had mentioned a family member who worked for a well-known pharmaceutical firm. Following up this lead, the field representative explored the idea of going to the pharmaceutical company for a possible gift-in-kind. The volunteer casually mentioned that she would ask her husband what the best way would be to approach the firm. Innocently inquiring about the role her husband played in all of this, the representative was told that the husband's brother was the chief executive officer of the firm. Valuable information like this was used by the nonprofit institution to obtain a gift for its work.

These examples of relational equity suggest that one of the principal tasks of a nonprofit strategist is to figure out how to maximize the long-term return to his or her organization's value investment as well as the value investment made by the donor, volunteer, or customer. It is at this juncture that success is truly realized. However, most large nonprofit organizations live instead within a "competitive tornado," where the tactical goal is to create any sort of marketplace advantage so as to beat out other like-minded organizations financially. Some organizations operating this way achieve great amounts of success in the short run in their endeavors. Left alone however, even successful short-term strategies can easily become viewed solely in economic terms by the organization, similar to the previously cited direct-mail example. When donors, customers, and volunteers are taken for granted and their values and aspirations are ignored tactically by an organization, the realized benefits that come from mutual engagement are left to chance and fate. Unfortunately, in some organizations, unless stakeholder collaboration is mandated by its leadership, this dialog becomes an activity the institution chooses to ignore.

BECOMING THE NONPROFIT STRATEGIST

Many nonprofit leaders still manage their teams in a manner akin to what M.I.T. professor Donald Schon calls in his book *Beyond the Stable State*, "dynamic conservatism," separating out divisions and their operations from each other with little resulting communication between each. Increasingly, however, the nonprofit causal field is discovering that virtually all the plans and decisions an organization's leadership makes have a value and a marketing implication. In fact, strategic planning ultimately becomes a series of marketing and value decisions that can cut across the boundaries of an organization's operations.

Asking how value fits into an organization's overall strategy should become a foundational question in everything an organization plans or attempts. Because it is increasingly hard for an organization to separate out *what* it does from the *way* it carries out operationally what it does, the question of *value* becomes even more important. In a stakeholder's mind, all that an institution undertakes easily becomes blurred into a representation of the entire organization. The classic example of this is the organization that provides great care to the market it is working within, but cannot get receipts out for two weeks to donors after it receives their gifts. These two operations become bundled—or inseparable—from each other in the mind of the donor. Success in one aspect of an organization's work does not guarantee that a stakeholder will forgive its bad operations in another. As institutions take the time to listen to their stakeholders, they readily find out that the relationships between all operations are viewed by stakeholders as positively or negatively contributing to each other. Professor Schon suggests, "Provider-customer relationships should be conceived not as one-way transactions but reciprocal constellations in which the parties 'help each other and help each other to help each other.'"[4]

It is easy to imagine how an institution following these suggestions could begin to realize possible new ways of designing its operations to bridge gaps between the way they currently operate and the way the marketplace might prefer it to operate. To bring these changes about,

- Organizational reengineering and program transformations would need to address how these changes would affect donors and customers in the marketing and program side of the agency's operations.

- The resulting impact of customer and donor concerns might in turn lead to program additions which might further lead the organization to a better competitive position within its causal industry.

- Taken together, the foregoing actions would ultimately involve new ways of thinking about how to deploy scarce organizational resources and secure additional ones.

How does a nonprofit manager *adopt the mind of the nonprofit strategist?* As previously suggested, some strategists start by first trying to outperform those institutions providing similar services, doing what other like-minded organizations are doing, only trying to do it better. Unfortunately, with so much promotional and programmatic imitation going on in the marketplace, marketing and organizational strategies can easily become mirror images of each other. Such approaches to strategy creation quickly become imitative and reactive, providing donors, customers, and volunteers with similar choices but not necessarily the ones they want. Nothing new is added to the value equation.

Instead, the job of the nonprofit strategist is to create new and exciting value opportunities for his or her agency's customers, donors, and volunteers by placing these individuals and their concerns at the center of what the nonprofit organization is doing. Anything of value to these individuals becomes the total collection of services and activities that are brought and presented to the stakeholder. The *exchange* between the two parties occurs as advantages to each are realized. The longer both work together and the more frequent the marketplace exchanges, the more both parties provide and realize evolving value from each other. The more frequently the marketplace changes, the more difficult, necessary, and important these exchanges become. However, by undertaking such actions, an organization quickly moves from becoming a "fast follower" to one that is viewed as a leader in the eyes of its stakeholders.

Reshaping Your Management Mind-Set

A lot of time is being spent at nonprofit seminars these days urging participants to become *transformational leaders.* By this, presenters typically mean to suggest that men and women should mobilize their teams of employees to create new, collective outcomes that help reinvent how their nonprofit organizations operate. In turn, these actions are supposed to help clarify where the institution is going. This focus on transformation—echoed by many consultants, seminars, and books—has resulted in literally hundreds of new leadership programs being created for consumption. Some, unfortunately, have had the result of providing an organization with a quick response for public-relations purposes rather than creating the necessary infrastructure and lasting capabilities needed to carry out initiatives long term. Institutions with good intentions and desiring transformation often find themselves saddled with programs whose design is murky and rudimentary in nature, neither costing much nor accomplishing much.

While it is unproductive to argue against the need for some of the elements organizational and leadership transformation programs may suggest and offer, still, for a great many organizations, these programs fail to address either the organization's current need and agenda or where it is attempting to navigate to in the future. To engage in transformational leadership is simply not enough for many organizations. Its transformational focus is often directed to the top of the management pyramid and not to the interior or exterior body of the organization. Good leadership is obviously important to the well-being of any institution, but changing leadership styles at the top is usually not the only variable needed to ensure that a nonprofit organization will continue to operate profitably into the unforeseen future. In fact, there are other variables that may be more important to the organization.

REAL-WORLD EXAMPLES

A marketing audit I undertook for an organization declared that the agency had great causal products but an insufficient infrastructure to carry out its programs. As a result, a discussion emerged inside the agency as it realized how important good systems, services, and structures were to its wellbeing. For years, the organization had operated on the premise that it was the absence of a superb marketing strategy that typically killed the growth potential within any struggling agency. As discussions progressed, the leadership of the institution began to believe that the absence of a finely tuned infrastructure could also kill their organization in the same way. Given the certainty that many of the societal issues the agency was dealing with seemed intractable to many of their stakeholders, the idea of building their organization in such a way as to be around for a long time became even more urgent.

Building a nonprofit organization for the future begins at the basement level in planning for the upcoming steps the institution needs to take, while systematically addressing gaps in staff, services, and skills to serve anticipated marketplace needs.

Operating As If the Future Mattered

How does an organization go about managing as though providing services in the future mattered? There are obviously a handful of good answers, and there are many ways to "win." However, among the various options available to managers today, one recurring pattern emerges that is common to many successful nonprofit organizations. In these institutions, managers at all levels take the time, expend the effort, and find the necessary resources to build a sustainable infrastructure architecture—a *market-centric machine*, if you will—behind the services the institution enacts. In other words, the leadership of these organizations first worry about how their programmatic ideas will be implemented, whether their ideas will achieve the results and answers they need in the context being addressed, and whether their agency programs are courageous, innovative, and daring enough. Going a step beyond these concerns, they concurrently take a hard look at their operating environments to determine what type of "infrastructure architecture" they have. Is theirs a fine-tuned, highly calibrated one that supports the current mission and is adaptable to the future, or is it not up to the task? Reviewing the backroom part of their operations while looking forward with their planned programs allows these managers a better chance at achieving their agency's aspirations.

Have you examined your organization's infrastructure? Unfortunately, success in the nonprofit world no longer comes solely as the result of being first in a causal market, or spending the most money on those you serve, or even having the highest-rated service programs. An institution must also have pliable operations and systems that allow its staff to act decisively when they decode changes in the stakeholder environment. They must provide the ability to outmaneuver competitors if necessary along with the organizational agility to respond appropriately and in a timely fashion.

The convergence of multiple competitors offering similar programs and products, the presence of smarter information technology, and real-time communication expectations from stakeholders are all leading many institutional executives to rethink the operations and practices of their corporate infrastructures. They are discovering—like their for-profit counterparts—that stakeholders are looking for more than what is trendy or fashionable. To build a base of collaborative customers, donors, and volunteers requires both constant vigilance and a routine reappraisal of the rules one is currently operating under. From the time an organization is first exposed to stakeholders to the end of the day when the lights are turned off, all decisions and activities must be thought through with the stakeholders in mind.

However, to be in tune with those who make up your stakeholder family is virtually impossible without first addressing how you will choose to support all you wish to do organizationally. When an institution decides to go about achieving its current service aspirations and future desires, it must decide whether it is going to run optimally at all levels of its operation: from the client and programmatic level, to the strategy the organization employs, to the efficiencies and systems it uses in its mailroom and its receipting operation. This beginning-to-end focus is sometimes called a *value chain*, and successful organizations seek to control and be concerned about it as much as possible.

Unfortunately, this is much harder to do than it sounds. Why? It was suggested previously in this text that a type of "dynamic conservatism" can be found in some organizations that limits their frame of reference. This frame can serve as a psychological and pragmatic barrier for many and may not allow leadership to see the need for equal and optimum performance across the entire organizational value chain. The actions that lead to this kind of "frame-breaking" may also not occur because of "the amount of work it takes" to holistically look at one's own organization. For example, taking the opinions of stakeholders seriously enough to affect operating decisions, or raising in organizational importance other parts of the institution to the level programming often symbolically holds, or forcing cross-functional teams to be a reality are all ideas that are important to institutions but not necessarily easy to implement.

There may also be historical or pragmatic reasons why a focus on elevating an organization's infrastructure in importance has not occurred. An agency's programming is typically what a nonprofit organization talks about publicly, and as leaders and development staff seek funds, programs are usually focused on and capture the "voice" and promotional spotlight of the agency. Consequently, programming typically enjoys a favored historical and cultural status inside an organization as opposed to the unseen operations (e.g., the mailroom, accounting, or human resource development). Many of these background operations simply never get talked about by those who represent an institution and can be portrayed as incidental to the success of an agency, especially to donors for whom these services seldom carry the same level of importance as other, more public works. Infrastructure operations like these are relegated to overhead and may not be viewed as worthy of interest by some.

Additionally, as some executives seek to create leaner organizations, they are using slash-and-burn tactics in the infrastructure area, resulting in quality losses and bad services that ultimately alienate stakeholders. Many executives feel free to do this psychologically and pragmatically because they themselves are not sure how important some systems and structures are in delivering their causal product to the markets they are serving.

In any discussion of the architecture of an organization's infrastructure, five macro issues emerge as critical to the discussion:

1. An organization's future agenda
2. The strategy and tactics an organization holds onto
3. The managerial need to integrate all aspects of its stakeholder operations

4. The communication and feedback system an organization operates with

5. The way these isolated operations are part of an interconnected cultural web

Each of these issues is explored in depth in Chapters 6 and 7.

NOTES

1. Ghoshal, Sumantra, Christopher A. Bartlett, and Peter Moran, "A New Manifesto for Management," Sloan Management Review, Spring 1999, vol. 40, no. 3, p. 17.
2. Brondmo, Hans Peter, The Engaged Customer (New York: HarperBusiness, 2000), p. 13.
3. Ibid., p. 13.
4. Schon, Donald, in the Forward of Richard Normann and Rafael Ramirez, Designing Interactive Strategy (New York: John Wiley & Sons, 1994), p. x.

REFERENCES

Godin, Seth, Permission Marketing (New York: Simon & Schuster, 1999).
Schon, Donald, Beyond The Stable State (New York: Random House, 1991).
DePree, Max, Leadership Is an Art (New York: Dell Publishing, 1989).

CHAPTER 6

Five Critical Issues: First, Know Where You Are Going; Second, Know How You Are Going to Get There

At a time when they need to be doing precisely the opposite, many nonprofit organizational leaders are increasingly focusing inward. Although there is already a chasm that separates some stakeholders from the organizations they are interested in, these nonprofit leaders are broadening this cavity by directing their resources internally toward preserving their organization's status quo. They are taking this step—perhaps unwittingly—by strengthening the systems their organizations have always used, redeploying the marketing and customer tactics that have traditionally been staged, and turning a blind eye toward those parts of their hierarchical structures that could become more competitively helpful if improved upon. Unfortunately, all of this is occurring at a time when our nation is filled with individualized interests that are dying to be satisfied, converging with many societal needs that are not being met using current methodologies. Instead of looking at the possibility of creating synergy in these situations and bringing diverse interests together, some organizational leaders have become increasingly remote and indifferent. "Let the marketing and development department deal with the people problems. I have to run the organization," they often say, either explicitly or covertly.

In all of this posturing, an implicit attitude is being suggested by these organizations and their leaders about stakeholders: "They" (the stakeholders) are here to serve "us" (the organization). Some institutions actually seem to incorporate this philosophy culturally and attitudinally in the way they work in the marketplace, with little thought given to organizationally accommodating opposite points of view or different ways of accomplishing critical tasks. However, these opposite points of view matter in the marketplace and make the existing attitudes of so many organizations untenable in the long run. In response to what some organizations seem to be saying by their actions, stakeholders are just as likely to suggest an opposite role for the nonprofit, "The nonprofit organization is here to serve my causal interests and concerns."

Sadly, what becomes lost in these polar-opposite viewpoints is the synergy and value that can be realized on behalf of societal needs through joint, deep-rooted partnering and relationship-building involving all parties. In fact, in dozens of organizations these relationships have been handled correctly and have become a series of meta-movements in their own right, as diverse parties combine forces creating fluid, interdependent partnerships that provide each other with support in pursuit of particular goals or causes.

A case in point: a key volunteer to an existing client has gone out of her way to solicit other individuals in the same profession to volunteer at this facility, and she has also become a donor, a product buyer, and a scholarship provider to the same organization. Over the past eight years she has sent 27 young people to this facility through scholarship help and has recruited six like-minded professionals to serve in a volunteer capacity. These volunteers, in turn, are buying organizational products, sending a new generation of individuals to this facility through scholarships, and recruiting new professionals to help. They have become a community and meta-movement within the larger organizational framework.

How does a nonprofit leader go about creating this type of relational, connective experience among many individuals? The initial steps start inside the organization and must concentrate on the essentials of how an institution operates and the logic it employs to get the agency's job done—that is, the organization's infrastructure architecture. It is in the logic an organization employs that allows real change to occur. There are five macro issues critical to the logic of an organization's infrastructure architecture that are discussed throughout the remainder of this chapter as well as in Chapters 7 and 8. These issues are

1. An organization's future agenda

2. The strategy and tactics an organization holds to

3. The managerial need to integrate all aspects of the organization's stakeholder operations

4. The communication and feedback system an organization operates with

5. The way the isolated operations are wrapped into an interconnected, cultural tapestry

Issue One: An Organization's Future Agenda

When young people are being disobedient, it is not uncommon for one parent to ask them, "Is this the way you would act if your father (or mother) were here?" In *The Fifth Discipline Handbook*, Peter Senge et al., ask a similar question: "If we act as we should, what would an observer see us doing? How would we be thinking?"[1]

"Does your organization have an agenda that takes the future into account? Do you know what needs to be done?" The overwhelming answer given by those when asked such a question is "yes!" Unfortunately, not all agendas are created equal. Upon further examination, some future agency agendas are seen to be built on fallacious assumptions, (i.e., ignoring the sea change in the conditions of leadership imposed by changes in the business environment). Even the most competent nonprofit executives have a problem navigating when this attitude is present. With most other agendas however, the idea of deciding what an organization is going to do and what it is not going to do in the future leads its leadership to grapple with the need to create a mission, a vision, and a goal statement (or statements). In essence, this amounts to creating a context for an organization to do service in the future. When organizations ignore both this intellectual effort and the routine wrestling process that often occurs early on in their corporate existence, they inadvertently deny stakeholders the opportunity to be inspired by the articulation of big-picture aspirations and objectives. From the mission, vision, and goals process flow the priorities of the organization and the strategies it will employ to achieve its dreams. Without such a process, an organization tends to focus inward and ignore pressing external issues that serve to drive it forward and bring about change and hoped-for success. In addition, the institution's leadership can easily be sidelined by issues that are important but not necessarily urgent. Priorities can become lost or postponed as issues not significant to the end goals of the organization take center stage. Peter Drucker, in his book *Managing the Nonprofit Organization: Principles and Practices*, noted that organizations had to first ask if what they were about to do advanced the ability of the organization to carry out its mission. This focus on end results starts with leadership looking outside-in rather than inside-out. This issue was so important that the well-known CEO Jack Welch also asked himself every five years, according to his biography, what needed to be done that was new and different.

As an organization creates a context for its future service, a big obstacle in the process can be the hopeful expectation that past conditions will continue as they were and stay the same into the future. This type of persistent, orthodox thinking about the organization's future can lead to the adoption of an equilibrium view of management and the environment, thereby nullifying diverse thinking and most likely resulting in possible future negative consequences. For example, a "don't rock the boat" mentality often becomes pervasive in these organizations, with managerial decisions that need to be made increasingly becoming designed to help protect agencies where they are, as opposed to where they may need to be.

It is easy to see how such thinking occurs. As any institution operates over time, it becomes automatic to get comfortable with ones' surroundings, trusting that conditions that occurred in the past will become a type of road map for what the agency hopes can occur again in the future. In this environment, customer, program, and marketing intelligence is typically centralized at the top levels of leadership. Hard agency issues are often avoided as bureaucracy replaces personal and departmental passion with predictable change, soon becoming the only type of change that is sought after. As a result, daily operations typically choose against discarding anything old for the perceived benefits of something new. Directives regarding programmatic fund development and marketing concerns come from the top and are automatically rolled out through the middle-management layer with little discussion.

Over time, a leadership team in this environment finds itself not responding to long-term social and economic forces. The team is psychologically simply unable to, as pervasive organizational mental maps become routine and mitigate against new thinking, discourage diverse thinking, and fail to challenge the status quo. For example, in working with a large East Coast conference center, the sales department had become so used to being reactive to the marketplace in processing rental groups that its management could not see any reason to take a proactive sales approach. The sales team had become order takers as opposed to order creators. Consequently, even though sales went down year after year, the sales team was frozen in a past reality when enough business came across the transom without their needing to worry about it. The vision for the organization's future had become tied in with notions of continuing the past.

A bounded organizational culture like this not only harms its enterprise but also begins to work against the stakeholder needs of collaboration, interdependence, and diversity as the institution tries to control as much of its destiny as possible by locking out possible divergent opinions, goals, and systems. Though the belief is that equilibrium will ultimately lead to marketplace advantage, instead what typically occurs is a condition McKinsey and Company associates and authors Richard Foster and Sarah Kaplan call "cultural lock-in."[2] This inability to change the dominant vision or mental maps an organization navigates by is governed through its fears of not being able to completely control the agency's future destiny.

Challenging an Organization's Vision in Order to Shape Its Destiny

Unlike some institutions that choose not to change, the majority of the philanthropic marketplace cannot be governed by these unchanging mental maps that are feeding biased visions of the future. Rather, because the marketplace is highly fluid and changes its loyalties easily in favor of different causes as it encounters new information and opportunities of service in areas that align with the personal values of potential stakeholders, agencies must exercise constant vigilance. Witness how the tsunami that devastated parts of Southeast Asia has also had the net effect of causing thousands of North American donors to redesignate and interrupt their gifts to agencies they supported in the past to engage this new opportunity for service.

The notion of "vision" in this type of changeable marketplace is increasingly governed by marketplace individuals who ask and then answer the question, "How will I satisfy my need for service in an area I am interested in?" Another example: a number of agencies who work principally on college campuses have found that after college life, students who have been involved with these institutions over the duration of their academic career, may continue their interest in the missional cause but their desire for involvement changes. This change in attitude is expressed in a number of different ways. Volunteering with the organizations in question may not be an option as new jobs are pursued by the graduates; the need for literature and information may change as individuals get married or begin to have children; and the general availability of these individuals to be involved also changes as their lives get fuller. Pragmatically and psychologically the lives of these recent graduates have been remade. While still agreeing with the core purpose of the nonprofit institution, most alumni nevertheless want to see it expressed differently within their own lives and values. In these situations, organizational vision should be neither dependent on current market conditions nor caught up in the past. New dexterity must be manifested in defining the organization's goals if it is to successfully involve these men and women meaningfully.

When I have been asked to speak at conferences with individuals of the Christian tradition, I often hear a verse quoted by speakers from the King James version of the Bible: "Where there is no vision, the people perish" (Proverbs 29:18). Vision is obviously crucial to the survival and success of many nonprofit organizations. To suggest otherwise would be unwise. Without a clear vision, organizations can flounder in the waters of competing needs. Unfortunately, some individuals quote statements like the one quoted and imply that vision must reside solely inside the mind of one or two leaders who decide what to do while the rest of the flock enthusiastically follows. When taken to the extreme, such a philosophy easily leads organizational leaders to adopt an egomaniacal stance in the marketplace, interpreting everything one way and only one way, often in light of past conditions and the whims of the director. As a result, an organizational culture of dependency and conformity ensues. Unfortunately, something of great consequence is lost within organizations in which this happens, particularly the synergy and innovative action that comes into play following the convergence of differing thinking promoted by similarly concerned individuals regarding a societal need that calls for intervention.

There are many ways individuals find or create a vision and subsequently use it as a basis or context for future goal-setting. In some cases a societal need may be so apparent that an organizational vision is presumed to be obvious and clear to everyone: Everyone should have enough to eat or enough water to drink. In other instances, an organizational vision is clearly borrowed or even plagiarized from another successful institution working in a similar area. Though this can lead to an inadequate and overly simplistic response to crucial societal needs, nevertheless it is much easier for some organizations to co-opt a vision rather than create something afresh.

Vision can also be created around an organizational personality and the dreams and aspirations one leader has, with the same individual typically becoming the focus for the organization, both in its fund development and in much of its programming. This is often seen in nonprofit institutions that utilize television or radio with a central personality as the dominant spokesperson, or in organizations that utilize a sports personality.

Some organizations may choose not to have a vision of the future, believing instead that their goal or goals can be arrived at in some not-too-distant future. Others, in the face of overwhelming societal needs, can't bring themselves to plan and try to work as hard as they possibly can every day. For them, the vision and the plan have become replaced by dedicated work.

A good share of the business literature still favors the notion that vision is created solely by the leader. Unfortunately, these are not easy times to be a leader and even tougher to be the sole "vision caster." Herein lies a problem with the way many administrators choose to manage. It is common for nonprofit managers to want to encourage a familial atmosphere in their corporate environments while still desiring to maintain a strong level of executive control.

Unfortunately, this mentality ignores what is happening to the rest of the business world, as thousands of corporate families, structures, and future plans are being destroyed through economic upheaval. As mutual commitments between company and employee have imploded in our society, the loyalty between the two has also faded and weakened. The nonprofit world is not immune from this phenomenon. Consequently, a new employee attitude has emerged, albeit more slowly in the nonprofit world, that demands both freedom of thought and a type of individual determinism. Men and women expressing this attitude want to shape their futures by having a say in creating them.

Some leaders see changes and emerging attitudes like these as "bad news" scenarios. They don't have to be. Rather, the likely possibility of discontinuous change in the makeup of most organizations will be more easily adapted to as different voices are enabled to speak and are listened to around the leadership table. As organizations are forced to evolve because of environmental and societal change, new voices often cross the boundaries of old mental maps more easily, illuminating new perspectives and ways of seeing and acting.

REAL-WORLD EXAMPLES

A group asked me for some consulting help, and I met the senior leadership team in an airport lounge. In the course of conversation, I asked the director what his aspirations were for the agency. His answers were passionate and articulate. When I asked the members of his leadership team how they felt about such a dominant vision, there was some quietly mouthed support for it. However, as I was driven to my hotel later, I asked the driver why the group support had not been greater for what was shared by the director. The young women said, "I have never heard where we were going as a team until today. I kind of knew, but I've never heard it explained. The team just works as hard as they can every day and hopes they're doing it right."

Knowing where you are going institutionally is a necessary part of creating a sustainable infrastructure architecture. However, this becomes useless information unless a leader and his or her team can define who you are and what your organization wants in terms of a marketplace presence in the future. Vision must translate into deeds. Without this, no organization can survive on mission and vision alone. Is there clear awareness of the future your organization desires to be a part of, or a stated value that marshals agency resources with specified action steps on how to achieve it? Is the dream clear, compelling, and directional? Does your organization know how it is going to keep track of its progress? Many organizations don't bother to answer these questions.

In fact, some nonprofit leaders wonder if knowing these answers is helpful and may view planning as a non–value added activity. Rather than looking at what needs to be done over the next 18 months or two years, these executives are as likely to say, "Just open your eyes; the need is in front of you." Within this expressed attitude of few expectations, there is little need for plans and checking results. And should planning occur in these organizations, it tends to be in the out-front program areas and not in hidden functions such as infrastructure or funding programs.

Though virtually every nonprofit agency leader has heard time and again that a vision and a plan are both essential, many leaders unfortunately, assume they already know where they are going. As suggested earlier, these men and women often feel angry if others do not immediately grasp the same strategic intent that they have or seem unwilling to take the same action steps.

When General Eisenhower purportedly suggested "plans are nothing; planning is everything," he seemed to say that planning is a process activity, not a three-ring binder filled with sheets of paper that sits on a shelf. Planning is to be engaged in constantly, with the plans being reviewed on a routine basis. Although this notion of a planning process is talked about at virtually all nonprofit seminars today, it seems to be missing from many day-to-day institutional activities. The adage that you must know what you want to do before you do it is being lost on many organizations. Again, there may be simple reasons for this. As was discussed in Chapter 5, it is easy for organizational plans to appear arbitrary in nature without a clear tie to a need being fulfilled. In such cases, planning appears to be unrealistic and downgrades the entire process, sometimes resulting in organizational or stakeholder disillusionment. In the case of the boardroom construction mentioned in Chapter 5, poor planning led to the wrong goals and the result was counterproductive to the organization.

Some organizations simply find it easier to start with a vision of an idealized future than to do the hard work of demonstrating to stakeholders how an improvement in the agency's infrastructure will lead to improved stakeholder services. This phenomenon is not hard to understand. Vision statements are fun to work on. In fact, one reason they are enjoyable is because they often are a projection of a time in the future that simply will never come to pass.

> We here at No More Hunger aspire to hire the very best workers and utilize cutting-edge technology to ensure all governments will work in harmony to allow those in hunger to be fed.

Though overstated here intentionally, visions grounded in fantasy are hard for workers to follow and share in emotionally. They can also lead to operational mediocrity. Why aspire to accomplish something organizationally that you really have no intention of trying to fund, achieve, or commit your organization to in any meaningful way? The absence of meaningful *targets* relegates the entire planning process to one of developing *wish lists* without being rooted in the realities of the organization or its environment. You can't set high growth goals and then simply hope for the best. Rather, you must have a fix on

- The type of causal business your organization thinks it is in and who your stakeholders and collaborators will be in this causal pursuit

- What success looks like for your cause from the organization's perspective and from the stakeholder's perspective
- The time frame and tactical steps that will be used to implement the agency's plan along with the costs for implementation
- How you will be accountable to your stakeholders and how you will communicate this accountability

Your organization's vision and plan ought to drive every aspect of your infrastructure, programming, and overall strategy. However simple or complex, these actions become the blueprints by which organizations navigate and impart a sense of identity and collective purpose. Drawn up correctly, these maps become a driving force in an organization and help determine a communal sense of where it will—and will not—go. Likewise, these priorities and aspirations become a benchmark against which the institution's strategy must perform. In short, defining them becomes the most important action an organization can take to ensure its future. What creates a good organizational environment in which to do planning? There are three critical issues that nurture this process:

1. An organization's leaders must have an expectation that should a plan go awry, they will confront the plan's poor performance and fix whatever is necessary to achieve what they are pursuing. Without a commitment to do what works and a commitment to fix what doesn't, planning becomes a waste of time. The unwillingness of organizations to confront poor performance may be the most important Achilles heel in nonprofit management today.

2. Tied to the cultural notion of not tolerating poor performance, an organization's leaders must have sufficient data intelligence so that they know how various programs and initiatives are functioning. Without the ability to inspect what an organization is doing and how it is doing it, there is little leverage managerially to expect great results. Factual data,

particularly as it tracks donors, customers, and volunteers and their values and relationships with the organization, is often in short supply in most agencies.

3. As an organization grows, it must change the way it manages and operates to accommodate its growth, and it must work harder on interfacing with and becoming sensitive to the public.

Issue Two: What Are Your Organization's Strategies and Tactics?

For many nonprofit organizations, their most important assets are no longer physical in nature. In fact, an agency's intangible assets, including its management and marketing strategy, what it hopes to accomplish in the service sector, and the plans and tactics it will use to get there, have all become increasingly important during the past several, highly competitive years.

Organizational planning is the benchmark against which a strategy must operate. Therefore, it becomes imperative that an agency's strategy be aligned with and supportive of where the institution is going. If not, it is most likely getting in the way of all that a leadership team hopes to accomplish in implementing its agency's vision.

It's easy for a strategy to go awry. A number of years ago a client had as its summer theme, "Walk your talk." Some nonprofit strategists need to take the truth of this adage to heart. These men and women operate as though the agencies they represent have already decided not to achieve their program or funding goals; instead, they are being misleading in how they tactically try to position their organizations. How does this happen? Strategists guilty of this pretense often operate as though their goal is to imitate a form of old-style press-agentry, trying to persuade a public perceived by the agency and its leadership as being gullible. By projecting big-picture visions, agency cultures that are not real representations, and environmental statements that are global in nature, strategists of this kind attempt to arrive at a deceptive goal by giving false and misleading impressions of what the organization is and where it is going. Strategists like these hope the public can easily be persuaded to their viewpoint. In fact, the opposite often occurs. Embedded in most nonprofit stakeholder cultures is a donor or customer segment likely to be sophisticated and street smart and also likely to use the falsehoods an organization promotes as a reason not to be involved with it.

Early in this chapter the suggestion was made that there is a widening gap between nonprofit organizations and their stake-holders. Why does this gap occur and what does an organization's strategy have to do with healing the resulting rift? The answers are important because stakeholders increasingly make choices about organizational support based on two levels: (1) how the stakeholder feels the nonprofit organization is performing in the marketplace and the impact it is or is not making and (2) the stakeholders' perception of how support of an organization allows them to express their personal values individually.

First, to attract stakeholder support, your cause must first be perceived as being worthy of an individual's interest. This is becoming an increasingly harder task for agencies to accomplish. Questionable actions by some of the most recognized charities in the world, the hyper-nonprofit competitive environments most agencies are a party to, and a sometimes sluggish economy have all contributed to creating a skeptical "show me" stakeholder environment. "Asking questions before they send money is now the norm for many nonprofit supporters. One of the questions being asked initially by many stakeholders—that a well-honed strategy must answer—is, "Will my gift be used for the reason the organization says it will be used for?" A question like this requires the reputation of a charity to be overwhelmingly positive and transparent.

Though there have been some well-publicized public relations problems during the past few years surrounding nonprofit institutions, of more damage to the entire philanthropic field may be the hundreds of charities that have been steadily crying "wolf" for years with no end in sight. Some of these agencies operate as if they have decided strategically that screaming "emergency" is the quickest way to funding success. This unfortunately has often proved true for dozens of agencies, especially in the short run. North American donors tend to be compassionate toward institutions in trouble. However, given the highly competitive environment many non-profit organizations find themselves in, those with a real or perceived history of past public-relations problems can create hesitation in the minds of would-be supporters. "Hesitation" typically leads to nonsupport. In the sustained-emergency culture that some agencies have put forth over long periods of time, donors and customers can begin to believe their gifts simply do not matter much and are not helping to reverse the critical situation the agency purports to be in. Consequently, individuals either begin to reduce their donation amount over time or stop giving altogether.

Second, your cause must also be perceived as being willing to collaborate with donors, customers, volunteers, and employees in helping them achieve their own personal value needs—what some sociologists call *expressive individualism.* Many stakeholders have resorted to a type of causal and agency sorting based on this need to express their personal value concerns and self-interest. Those institutions they feel comfortable with are awarded their involvement. Those that are not perceived as a good fit, are not. The stated cause and the societal need the agency in question projects often figure tangentially in the decision to help or not. As with the philosophical framework many case statements employ, most stakeholders need to see meaning and hope in what they do in a world that is often hard to figure out and cope with. Desiring to feel both different from the world around them and to be a part of something that matters, stakeholders want to feel preferred and sought after in order not to be consumed by the real or perceived chaos around them.

Organizations that do not take these value concerns into account within their strategies often find a "value gap" between those inside the agency looking for funding and support and the external prospective supporters and volunteers they are targeting. There may also be a much larger widening gap between the organization and many other possible stakeholder audiences, including employees and suppliers. The reason for this is relatively simple. If organizations are not disposed to collaborate institutionally or to study those they must collaborate with to uncover their value systems in order to target their messages, they are most likely to display this non-collaborative attitude to many audiences. Unlike previous generations of nonprofit agency leaders who often felt they needed to worry only about the parts of their audience that gave financial or customer support to the organization, today's nonprofit strategists must deal with a much larger audience than simply the traditional segments that give donations or buy agency products.

In fact, a strategist must go beyond the traditional "four P's" (product, price, promotion, and place) that have served nonprofit marketers successfully for years and are often talked about at marketing seminars. Instead, one must look to a new strategy definition of creating value across the entire value chain an agency works within, including supportive stakeholders at all levels inside and outside the agency. Each audience must be considered as an important target within the strategy equation.

Why this need for change? The aforementioned alignment issue is one reason. The causal task facing most nonprofit organizations is simply too big for any agency to assume it can afford to lose a possible supporter in the marketing process and go on as though nothing has changed. Casualties will occur regardless. However, unless organizations act as though every person is perceived as important and needed, they can too easily adopt the notion that "you can't please everyone" as an excuse. It may appear overly obvious to stress this, but within most agencies the annual rates of donor dropout are horrific, often within the 35–60% range or higher. Unfortunately, in recent nonprofit seminars and many current marketing texts, stakeholder retention strategies have become one of the great undiscussed issues. Acquisition strategies, however, are another matter. It's as though many pundits have assumed that there is an unending supply of donor prospects in the United States. This has had the net effect of allowing many nonprofit leaders to spend less time worrying about taking care of their constituents.

Why do individuals lapse in their support of certain agencies? Certainly the overly communicated society we live in is a major reason for this problem. Readers, listeners, and watchers are exposed to more media than they once were. One media specialist in the political realm does not retire a commercial until would-be voters have seen it 12 times as opposed to 5 times 10 years ago.[3] His reason for this change is that it is simply tougher to create levels of awareness and memorability. Another reason for stakeholders to lapse is the increase in the number of causal competitors offering similar nonprofit services and products, thereby creating more stakeholder choices and increasing competing demands for the attention of would-be customers and donors. A third critical reason is the splintering of the mass audience into fragments or narrow subgroups that require increased message specialization to reach effectively. Many organizations choose to ignore this fact and continue to send broad-based appeals. To close such gaps and create strategic alignment, organizations must view each possible audience member as someone to be nurtured, studied, listened to, and worked with in a manner such that mutual productivity is created. Without this underlying attitude within nonprofit management, gaps will occur.

Isn't this equally true with agency employees? There might be similar reasons for an agency's employees not aligning themselves with the organizations they work with. These might include a perceived lack of importance in the jobs they're being asked to do, an unwieldy agency bureaucracy that has created slow decision-making, or a lack of employee ownership in the vision of the organization. Again, without symmetry between the concerns of employees and the organization, future trouble can be predicted.

Regardless of reason, if a gulf opens up between an organization and any of its stakeholders, it is unfortunately happening at a time when it is the relationships and communication strategies an organization uses to create interconnectedness that matter strategically. Creating two-way interactivity with as many stakeholders as possible throughout an organization's value chain and using personal and mass communication tactics to gain and nurture this relational tapestry helps create long-term stakeholder retention and contributes to the equity a brand enjoys (i.e., its value beyond its physical assets).

In light of this, it is surprising that many nonprofit organizations do little in the way of strategically managing their brand equity. Rather than first looking at all the components of their service operations and recognizing that this intangible side of the organization is important because it allows individuals to buy into an organization's vision and identify with the agency's aspirations, many organizations are placing their marketing emphasis elsewhere in more traditional ways. Places of worship routinely face this issue. It is not unusual for them to face uphill battles in funding their operations. When donations are down, the economy is usually blamed. In the ensuing discussions about what to do regarding the decline, typically what is left out of the discussion is whether parishioners are satisfied in their worship experience. Are the programs being instituted ones that people want? Is the service or preaching inspiring and helpful? If these questions are not answered, houses of worship typically see a decline in both donations and membership.

Even though many nonprofit organizations now spend more time improving their promotion, pricing, and asking strategies than ever before, these supportive improvements in and of themselves do not necessarily create or build strong equity. Marketing concerns have caused many organizations to take a hard look at their causal products and improve their delivery and performance systems; these are good steps, but they simply do not go far enough. Something more is needed.

Measuring Success and Failure

When a nonprofit organization has as its primary mission, to "help collegians develop spiritual insight," or to "alleviate psychological suffering wherever it is encountered," how do such mission-driven organizations measure success and failure? Many for-profit organizations have a straightforward means of measuring marketplace success or failure in terms of financial profit and loss, but for the most part, nonprofit organizations have not developed a uniform rigorous methodology to do so. Indeed for some organizations, success and failure measurements might never be adequately forthcoming. Dr. W. Edwards Deming understood the difficulties of purely numerical evaluation and often quoted the director of statistical methods for the Nashua Corporation, Dr. Lloyd Nelson, who stated, "The most important figures needed for the management of any organization are often unknown and indeed unknowable."[4]

Success and failure can be easy to measure depending on an organization's reason for existence. For example, an organization that provides meals to those needing them may choose to simply measure the number of meals they serve and the dollars they raise to cover the cost of providing the meals. This commonsense approach allows the organization to tally numbers as basic indicators. This cost ratio and utility approach, however, may not go far enough for some of today's stakeholders, who may be looking for mission and progress indicators. When Albert Einstein noted, "Sometimes what counts can't be counted, and what can be counted doesn't count," he was most likely not talking about nonprofit success or failure or stakeholder strategy and value creation. However, sophisticated donors, customers, and volunteers have become preoccupied with value creation and other important strategic issues. Nonprofit strategists have had to take into account not only their need to measure the stewardship of their organizations but also the changing notions of what success or failure means to many stakeholders. Unfortunately, some notions of success and failure have come into conflict with the definitions many organizations still hold to and use. When asked, for example, to define what a successful strategy should look like, nonprofit leaders often have little to say about the subject as it relates to donors, customers, employees, and volunteers. For many of these leaders, measures of strategic success are typically about achieving the core goals of the mission as expressed in financial terms and not necessarily about serving or satisfying stakeholders or being concerned about the tactics employed to achieve the mission.

This, of course, is where the strategic rub occurs in some agencies. Success may be defined by stakeholders differently than the way the organizations they are interested in are defining it. As far as the stakeholder is concerned, strategic success may have as much to do with the organization's being centered on values the stakeholder holds most dear as with the areas its mission is focused on. Providing this understanding of the stakeholder's need for duality can become not only an important distinction in the life of an organization but its most important strategic marketing weapon. When a stakeholder's supportive concerns are seriously listened to and are incorporated into an organization's thinking and operations, as well as being nurtured by strong communication and relation-ship-management strategies, they become the means by which an organization begins to break through the communication noise that surrounds most stakeholders and begins to establish a strong brand equity. If it fails to take the time to demonstrate the values and personality a stakeholder wishes to express through an agency, an organization's causal products may not sell as well in the future.

Knowing what success looks like both for the institution and stakeholder becomes important in this equation. Having a family of measures that concern not just revenue and "counting" goals tied to institutional progress but as well the progress being made toward fulfilling the mission along with the tactics and means being used to get the organization there is key. The clearer the goal being discussed and the narrower its mission, the easier it is to have stakeholder discussions centered on measurement. Independent sales consultant George H. Peeler notes,

> Almost too much information is being pushed towards the customer for conscious consideration, much less logical processing. What has become the Information Age has the potential of becoming the Misinformation Age. Confusion can appear to reign. Drenched with information, customers often feel bewildered. They are beginning to search for safe havens represented by products and by vendors that can be depended upon and that allow a respite from the clamor of the marketplace.[5]

Stakeholder equity doesn't occur solely because an agency does a good job with its marketing and communication strategy. Rather, it occurs and begins to exist in the hearts and minds of an institution's stakeholders when they see their value needs fulfilled in the day-to-day workings of a nonprofit institution they care about. Unlike many popular sentiments, relationship equity with an organization is not born directly as a result of printing vision statements on brochures, of creating pricing or donation strategies that are attractive, or even of making strong improvements in the performance of an agency's causal products. Stakeholder equity comes into being when marketing strategists focus on the soft, relational side of their organization's business as well as its harder businesslike edge and allow all parts of the organization to work toward accomplishing its vision and core mission. Unless this synergy takes place, marketing strategies lose their efficiency in helping an organization build its brand. When organizational branding issues are relegated by strategists to the level of secondary concerns, the notion of working to retain stakeholders for long periods of time by building long-lasting and profitable relationships also suffers.

A certain level and class of information is critical to building an institution's brand and retaining its stakeholders for long periods of time. Virtually everyone agrees there has been an information revolution in our society. As noted, however, some now feel there may be too much information available. Although more marketing information is available to nonprofit organizations than ever before, they have often been slow to utilize it to build strong relational bonds and increase donor retention. Managing information must be at the core of what strategy managers do. At a time when organizational equilibrium is almost impossible to sustain, strategy innovation and adaptation gained from what you know about your stakeholders is critical in dealing with them in a discontinuous world and becomes vital in providing new ways to create value for them.

How is this accomplished? Internally, strategy managers must be on the lookout for information that not only shares financial news but looks at both marketing and strategy initiatives as well as ongoing program successes and failures. In this way, information management becomes a crucial benchmark for existing organizations to recapture past successes and allows them to create a stronger marketplace presence, even though they might lack commensurate resources to do so widely. For example, if an organization is beginning to mature in its life cycle, tactical information must become critically embedded within its strategy. This information must do an excellent job of embodying the agency's story in a manner that gives stakeholders reasons to continue supporting the organization. Further, in a new or recently launched nonprofit organization, delivering what stakeholders feel is fair value for the dollars they donate or the time they invest is something that information flows must be directed to as the means by which to operate.

In the for-profit world, share price and profits are clear indicators of success and failure; the path is not as clear, however, in the nonprofit world. There is a need to manage beyond the numbers—but how? To build a more effective strategy there are five critical issues a strategist must address through his or her information systems.

1. A strategist must first decide what is going to be measured organizationally. As part of this critical decision, management should decide to measure both the initiatives that lend themselves to easy measurement practices (such as donations) and the intangible areas that are often harder to measure (how the program directors are doing). Having determined this, organizational leadership must create a list of key indicators in descending order so that the most important information is captured first. Without doing so, an organization that has not done much measurement will find itself quickly stymied by trying to measure as many things as possible without necessarily having the wherewithal to make the information actionable for management.

2. A marketing strategist must then decide, in conjunction with an agency's leadership, who in the organization is going to see the information? If information gathering is left assigned to all department heads with little in the way of managerial teeth in the directive, then meaningful information gathering will not happen. Increasingly, larger and more complex nonprofit organizations within some causal industries are finding they have to hire an information officer to help them manage both their organization's information flow and the security behind the dispersal of key data, help determine the timeliness of the information dispersal, and help prioritize what is going to be measured in what sequence.

3. It is not wise to implement the first two steps and then forget this third step: How will the information gathering process

be used to create more value for key stakeholders? Will it find its way into annual reports, into quality-control charts for program leaders, into donor data that helps field representatives do their jobs, or into any number of other areas? Will the information be actionable enough so that the parent organization can change its strategy should the data dictate it? Clear and actionable data tied to measurable goals will move stakeholders and secure their support in a way that lofty mission statements will not.

4. Data that is gathered in an organization must be timely, as specific as possible, prescriptive, and presented in a financial framework. Data must be timely if it is to have an impact on an organization's actions. Strategies are imitated so quickly in the marketplace by competitors that the cycle time for data does not leave room for it to be old. In addition, data that is collected must address specific parts of an organization if the information is to be acted on. The more specific the data being gathered, the more the data can be looked at by managers and become a guide to decisions they may have to make. The absolute best guide that data can provide takes the form of clear-cut recommendations—for example, "By taking this step as opposed to that step, we will deliver more value to our donors and should retain them on an average of 11 months longer than we are currently."

5. Peter Drucker observed, "All the data we have so far, including those provided by new tools, focus inward. But inside an enterprise—indeed, even inside the entire economic chain—there are only costs. Results are only on the outside."[6] If a nonprofit organization is really going to benefit from the information revolution, then it must both create an internal data footprint and work to integrate this information with continuous, real-time market information. In fact, forward-thinking nonprofit organizations are looking at their

compensation plans with the need to create long-term stakeholder creation in mind. Internal data, created in isolation, does not help focus an agency externally, whether the issue is funding sources, financial markets, employee markets, or customer segments.

Marketing information should be one of the pillars an organization rests on, determining how well it is working in realizing its aspirations. An agency's organization of its information system should be thought of as important enough that it becomes viewed as an asset supporting all the agency's actions.

Knowing where you are going (Issue One) and how you are going to get there (Issue Two) are both critical and important questions. However, the answers to these questions reach their potential usefulness in providing a road map of sorts for an organization only when they are integrated with each other and with other critical infrastructure systems. Chapter 7 begins with Issue Three and shows how managerial integration must take place; it continues by demonstrating how an organization's cultural and communication web becomes part of the glue that binds all of these disparate pieces together into a meaningful whole (Issue Four).

NOTES

1. Senge, Peter, A. Kleiner, R. Ross Roberts, and B. Smith, The Fifth Discipline Fieldbook: Strategies and Tools for Building a Learning Organization (New York: Doubleday, 1994), p. 302.
2. Foster, Richard and Sarah Kaplan, Creative Destruction (New York: Currency, 2001), p. 79.
3. Farhi, Paul "More Media, Less Message," Washington Post National Weekly Edition, June 21–27, 2004, p. 11.
4. Peeler, George H., Selling in the Quality Era (Cambridge: Blackwell Business, 1996), p. 8.
5. Ibid., p. 35.
6. Boulton, Richard E.S., Barry D. Libert, and Steve M. Samek, Cracking the Value Code (New York: HarperBusiness, 2000), p. 219.

■ REFERENCES

Drucker, Peter, *Managing the Nonprofit Organization: Principles and Practices*, (New York: HarperCollins, 1990).

Drucker, Peter, *The Five Most Important Questions You Will Ever Ask About Your Nonprofit Organization* (San Francisco: Jossey Bass, 1993).

Welch, Jack with SuzyWelch, *Winning* (New York: Collins, 2005).

CHAPTER 7

Integration and Communication: Issues Three and Four Continued

Implied throughout the pages of this book is the notion that traditional nonprofit marketing needs to be rethought in the light of stakeholder values. Within the hypercompetitive world that most organizations find themselves a part of, a growing gap has emerged between what nonprofit marketing should look like and the practices many organizations currently follow. In Chapter 6, Issues One and Two gave foundational reasons why an institution has to know both where it is going and the strategies it plans to use to get there along with the benefits these actions present to stakeholders. Though these two concerns are important to every institution, unfortunately they cannot in and of themselves help an organization successfully compete in a crowded and competitive universe. There is a third issue that nonprofit leaders must wrestle with in light of stakeholder concerns.

ISSUE THREE: THE MANAGERIAL NEED TO INTEGRATE ALL ASPECTS OF STAKEHOLDER OPERATIONS

Many nonprofit organizations routinely operate with a number of internal constraints that impose limits on their performance in the marketplace. One critical constraint is the uncertainty an agency may have in reaching its institutional goals. What explains the relative failure of most institutions to create an effective strategic scenario in which goals are met? Part of this problem is that nonprofit agencies and their managers have great difficulty clearly and consistently defining what "winning" means in terms of reaching a goal. When this uncertainty is coupled with a shifting economic environment, the situation often leads to roadblocks in formal planning. As a result, rather than an organization asking holistically, "What are we able to create collectively?", turf battles often occur between departments about goals and how to reach them. Without the discipline of cross-functional planning, internal divisions can easily result in chronic failure to keep donors, customers, and volunteers central to the agency's mission. Lack of corporate discipline regarding an agency's marketing and service objectives coupled with the absence of adequate operational capital can lead organizations in and out of this difficult situation. In other words, integration of effort is nonexistent.

Unless these managerial issues are attacked in a company-wide fashion, managerial integration, a critical and vital source of competitive advantage available to most nonprofit organizations, evaporates. What is meant by *integration*, and why is integrating stakeholder operations important?

Within the nonprofit management context, integration recognizes that the world is made up primarily of relationships. It speaks to the consistency of effort an agency puts forth in managing various relationships through its external communication coupled with mutual interactivity with stakeholders. This consistency of effort also includes the internal practices of cross-functional planning and departmental dialog. The ultimate goal of these business practices is to increase the strength and trust of an agency's name and brand in the minds of stakeholders. This helps to generate the desire within individuals to interact with the organization and bring needed resources to the table. In addition, more service opportunities tied to the institution's mission will be created.

For some managers, the notion of integration appears to work against the parallel notions of decentralization and being nimble in the marketplace. Unfortunately, it is the pervasive lack of managerial and marketing integration within many nonprofit agencies that has typically had this negative market effect, not its presence. When organizational departments and their managers do what is right in their own eyes and claim small niches in the marketplace, the notion of large-scale stakeholder collaboration can get lost, as can the synergy gained by an institution and its supporters when they share a central vision, commensurate brand values, and identity.

This lack of synergy is often seen within larger nonprofit organizations operating nationwide or worldwide. Depending on an agency's geographic location, different causal products or processes may be operating, that do not resemble neighboring areas of operation within the agency. Though an organization's vision may not be *centralized* (proceeding from the top of the organizational chart down through the institution), nevertheless it is vision and integration that must woo the bulk of an agency's stakeholders through their understanding of its brand and cause. If there is not a similar standard and understanding across geographical boundaries, organizations begin to lose focus on the task at hand (among other things), and this ultimately leads to a dysfunctional strategic effort.

Integration of processes and effort is critical. because it takes into account the marketplace *power* today's donors, volunteers, and customers hold, a power previous generations may not have felt they had or could utilize. With the ability of virtually any stakeholder to use the Internet to access and acquire all sorts of service and causal information, as well as the presence of numerous similarly positioned philanthropic choices, the nonprofit stakeholder has gained tremendous marketplace leverage and power. To relate to this "new consumer," many nonprofit organizations are being forced to change the nature of their operations and the way they speak to stakeholders, moving from a communications and marketing environment that is outbound in nature and tells the nonprofit consumer how to act and when to give or volunteer to one that deals with stakeholders on their own terms. Northwestern University professor Don E. Schultz writes, "To market in the customer-driven marketplace of the twenty-first century, the firm must start with customers and prospects, their needs and wants, their potential, and their opportunities and integrate all the marketing and communication activities."[1]

Integration of effort is also important to the stakeholder because of its ability to improve the delivery of institutional services and capabilities. Service integration can help agencies become truly market driven by allowing superior processes and services to be delivered to stakeholders through distinct organizational and departmental patterns that exploit their abilities to relate to various markets. Being stimulated through internal organizational dialog to both identify and deliver an agency's distinctive capabilities, institutions can begin to create exemplars of coordination and service delivery that are important to the stakeholder. Emphasizing external objectives that are compelling to these men and women (such as donor satisfaction or receipt order processing time), the capabilities then become the basis for control and measurement systems that are important to the donors' sense of stewardship and the customers' sense of value. Unfortunately, the interdepartmental dialog occurs infrequently in hierarchical situations where managers control silos of power and do not share information.

However, what if managers were forced to or expected to engage in this dialog?

REAL-WORLD EXAMPLES

For example, in many nonprofit organizations program officers do not typically concern themselves with receipting issues, and receipting officers usually do not concern themselves with the vast majority of programmatic issues. Typically, the information is not readily available to each type of officer and the concerns are not within their purview. Consequently, the viewpoint of one supervisor does not seem important to the other supervisor in charge. What if both parties were mandated by their senior leadership to make the delivery of receipts a distinctive capability within the organization as opposed to being simply an activity undertaken by one department? Going a step further, what if the goal of this exercise was to create superior customer value through the receipt process? Is it not possible that the insights of both these supervisors, taken together, could create a truly market-driven receipting process that involved new strategic thinking, resource allocation, and stakeholder values? Might new processes be developed if the entire receipting function is examined through new eyes, as opposed to being regarded simply as an isolated departmental activity?

The possibilities for superior service become even more endless when organizational processes are viewed through both new internal agency eyes and the eyes of external stakeholders, suggesting what brings value to them personally. What might the effects be for an agency that, finding itself in a competitive environment, may not be engaging in cross-functional planning or making a serious effort to integrate all of its managerial and marketing programs?

Multiple negative issues can occur simultaneously. Perhaps the most salient and apparent one occurs as a direct result of the number of nonprofit organizations and similarly focused institutions that have rapidly proliferated during the past several years. With so many agencies sharing similar causal behaviors, it is hard for any one nonprofit organization that does not integrate its effort to maintain much of a competitive advantage over long periods of time, especially as the marketplace begins to commoditize the number of agencies engaging in similar sets of services and causal programs.

REAL-WORLD EXAMPLES

For example, in advising a religious group that specializes in working among collegians, I found more than 14 other groups offering similar types of services, meetings, and causal products aimed at comparable demographic groups on one campus. How would any unintegrated organization with an operating style that was similar to so many others compete and survive in such an environment? Unfortunately, in today's crowded marketplace many institutions don't.

In the earliest days of this collegiate organization's life cycle, it may have been the only such group operating on some campuses. In a single-operator environment, loyalty to a group could have been expected from both college customers and interested donors and volunteers who were not in school. These circumstances no longer exist for this organization. Collegiate customers looking for certain spiritual products now have many choices. In some academic environments the events, meetings, publications, and structures in place—in essence, the "causal products"—have become commodities in themselves, with very little difference between the various offerings. For the donor looking to support such a spiritual endeavor, there are an equal number of product choices. With causes and products so similar, both donor and customer have the ability to switch organizational allegiances at will because there is little risk to them in doing so.

When the campus organization finally decided to integrate its marketing and management effort, did the decision make any difference to the agency's competitiveness? The answer was "Yes"; operational events changed in the following ways:

- Through aggressive dialog and equally aggressive listening to its collegiate customer base, the organization learned how to better plan and operate on campuses, thus managerially tightening up its mission. Consequently, its marketing program gained in stature and efficiency.

- Based on in-depth dialog and aggressive listening to its collegiate customers, the type of communication the organization was sending to prospective customers was revised to become more consistently tied to the values and concerns the targeted market exhibited.

- By virtue of taking the first two suggestions to heart organizationally, the organization began to produce strong relationships across the targeted demographic customer base. Learning as much as possible about its customers not only increased the organization's credibility within the target group but also began to have the net result of retaining these customers longer.

- Interdepartmental dialog within the agency also increased. Had the organization asked, "How do we retain our collegiate customers longer?" some years ago and then seriously sought the answer, it might have been forced to put together some of the best minds in the agency from across multiple departments to come up with anything other than simplistic answers. This would have then created operational and cross-functional implications across communication, research, marketing, and database lines of authority. It might also have forced inter-agency dialog in a much more timely fashion.

- Departmental isolation was replaced by coordination as the organization strove to put a total communication program in place to create a stronger brand image across college campuses.[2]

To succeed in the commodity environment it found itself in, the campus agency had to show not only that it was motivated by its mission but that this mission had the values of the stakeholders in mind. This outcome then became the heart of the organization. However, without each department working closely in unison and supporting the others in pursuit of this common goal, such an outcome would be unlikely.

Unfortunately, the lack of corporate integration leads naturally to other critical issues that grow out of the hypercompetitive environments many nonprofit agencies find themselves in. With so many institutions operating throughout North America (more than twice as many exist today than in 1977), the communication density and din that donors, customers, and volunteers have to attend to is overwhelming. As a result of this strain, increasing numbers routinely tune out the messages organizations send them. Unfortunately, these individuals have not just become more resistant to fund-raising and advertising messages, but more resistant to the ideas and information these messages seek to convey.

This communication problem takes on an added complexity within institutions that have multiple divisions that, with little thought of schedule coordination, talk directly with overlapping stakeholder audiences. When these divisions create and send out their own communication streams—typically with little thought to being consistent in style, visual content, and message with communications from the rest of the organization—they often sound and look like separate, competing agencies to the consumer. Integration of organizational communication and effort appears nonexistent. In addition, not much effort is usually taken by these divisions to define themselves as part of a much larger whole. Consequently, the consumer has another reason to shut down mentally, often viewing the advertising communication and the parent agency that has allowed the messages to be sent in a negative light.

What are some solutions to these multiple problems?

Not surprisingly, the solutions start with the consumer. Nonprofit organizations that put their stakeholders first soon realize every action their organization takes or fails to take gives an impression of the agency to the stakeholder. The sum of all of these combined impressions creates a brand image that donors, customers, and volunteers have of the organization. Unless agency leaders think through how they will coordinate and integrate all the points of contact they have with their various audience segments, message consistency is lost, as is the chance to create a strong emotional impression in the stakeholder's mind.

Unfortunately, there is a misguided notion some nonprofit leadership teams choose to live with when it comes to integrating their agency's stakeholder efforts. For these directors, integration of effort has never been much of a concern or problem. They know precisely when every brochure and promotional piece is being produced by their organization. They can tell you the drop dates of every direct-mail piece and its intended audience, as well as the dates of their special events and the names of those who will participate. In addition, they can usually recite the names of many of the agencies and individuals that are partners with the institution. From the perspective of these leaders, their entire communication effort is integrated.

However, integration for these organizations lies solely in the mind of their directors but not in the areas where it is most needed and most beneficial. Organizational integration is not solely concerned with communication efforts and scheduling, though these are obviously important issues. Rather, integration concerns itself first with the organizational entities that are concerned with stakeholder satisfaction and service, and looks to span the boundaries between the various departments that serve the stakeholders. The goal of integration is to take the knowledge each department has about and the goals it has set for the stakeholders and provide a unifying lifeline between them and the organization. Ideally, every organizational service is part of this discussion.

Fund-raising, sales, data mining, donor and customer fulfillment, promotional scheduling, registration, and event planning
are just some of the functions that should be aligned and then
integrated.

Discussions about integration within nonprofit organizations
often break down because the assumption is made that integration is
precisely and solely an internal, organizational issue. As we have
seen, it is not. Integration is also an external stakeholder issue. Just as
there must be system linkages internally to make integration work,
there must also be a seamless web of social activities and relationships
that link stakeholders to the organization and to each other.
Unfortunately, the issue of organizational control comes into play
for many institutions at this point. In such instances, agency
leadership teams may function with both actual and intentional top-
down controls. The reason behind this operational stance is that
leaders are often afraid of having non–agency designated stakeholders speak for the organization or become its advocates in case
something is said or done that either reflects badly on the
organization or conflicts with an operational position. In extreme
cases, management may view the majority of stakeholders as being
irrational or simply not knowledgeable about the organization.

The resulting lack of integration in these circumstances has more
to do with agency actions than with stakeholders. Of course, an
alternative approach would have the unique set of organizing lenses
that guides stakeholder values to be well known and integrated into
the agency's DNA. In fact, the two value groups—external
stakeholders and the internal organization—would mirror each
other in belief systems, and these would be known to each other.
From this synergy would emerge a competitive advantage as the
agency's "personality," its emotional convictions, and its values
matched those of its supporters and vice versa. The more in sync the
internal agency and external stakeholders became with their
collaborative value sets, the fewer mistakes would be made in
the marketplace.

Managerial and marketplace integration is ultimately important for one very large reason and for a host of supportive smaller ones. The large reason is simply this: Nearly all nonprofit agencies do not have enough resources to be able to achieve their core mission. They do not have enough money, people, donors, volunteers, management, or staff. Yet, many organizations persist in fighting with themselves in the marketplace because of a lack of cross-functional integration, despite the disadvantages of so doing. The societal and global issues most nonprofit agencies are trying to correct are simply too large and too diverse to permit them to continue to this pattern and go it alone. More is often better in causal work. More collabora-tion, more donors, and more volunteers are needed by almost every institution. To address this need, message and management integration can become a distinguishing set of organizational metrics that can guide deci-sion-making processes and help to achieve this goal.

Issue Four: The Communication and Feedback System an Organization Operates With

One of Britain's top management writers, Charles Handy, suggested that businesses don't work unless they become communities.[3] Communities are often built on shared systems, procedures, and cultures, created in part by messages that move their infrastructures and citizenry in a strategic direction. However, if communities—and businesses—focus solely on transactions that take place with each other, they will not prosper and survive over time. There must be more that holds them together.

In business communities the catchall phrase for this bonding agent is customer relationship management (CRM). The success of these communities depends on high-involvement relation-ships that are based on understanding, attracting, and keeping stakeholders and organizations together for the long term. To work, these relationships must function in such a way that they clarify and untangle for each other where an organization's vision and strategy are headed. Issue Three spoke to achieving organizational integration, an important step in building an institution that keeps stakeholders in mind. However, to achieve what Handy was talking about, integration must also be coupled with and be dependent upon good agency communication that is strategic in nature.

Together, these dual practices of integration and good communication lead to stronger stakeholder relationships. In turn, these affiliations induce alignment within an agency's strategy and help create commensurate action, the end goal of any good communication program. When integration and communication are further strengthened by the opportunity for consistent feedback, these actions yield potentially new ideas and can lead to mutual understanding, cooperation, and affinity. Taken together, these practices enable both elevated stakeholder retention from the organization's perspective and mutually, longer organizational retention from the stakeholder's perspective.

For a communication program to be focused on stakeholders and organizational strategy is nothing new. It is however, a necessary antecedent to any serious dialog regarding communication between agency and stakeholder in society's hypercompetitive world. Today, no matter where a nonprofit communication director turns—events, direct mail, telemarketing, the Internet—the story is much the same. All media channels are crowded and, therefore, increasingly less effective in delivering a nonprofit agency's message. The most obvious upshot of this dilemma is that it can be more expensive to talk to some stakeholders, particularly as agencies modify their messages by segment. Therefore, as audiences splinter into more narrow niches and organizations segment their messages around specialized media, only a few communication rules seem to still apply.

First: Communication Programs Need to Be about Stakeholder Retention

There is a quantifiable difference between the costs to acquire a new donor or customer and those to maintain an existing one. Retention (some prefer to substitute the word *loyalty*) makes abundant sense as a strategic imperative and the end goal of any good communication program. Nonprofit interaction must be aimed at retaining customers, donors, and volunteers while strategically building relationships with them for as long as possible. Why?

The simple answer is that it is more economical for a nonprofit organization to retain friends for a longer period of time than to have to routinely find new ones. Entropy is the inherent tendency of relationships. A number of authors suggest that it costs about five times as much to attract new customers as it does to maintain the existing ones.[4] Not only does the action of maintaining its stakeholders make sense when talking about the costs of acquisition, but the longer an agency's benefactors are retained, the more the benefactors will share their time and money with the organization they're interested in. Long-term benefactors give more philanthropic dollars cumulatively and therefore become more profitable to an institution. They also volunteer more, frequently become better customers, and often unashamedly tell others about the cause and organization they are supporting. In addition, they are more forgiving and willing to overlook mistakes the institution may have made. However, when chronic agency abuse or errors occur, long-term benefactors are equally as likely to vent their frustrations and tell numerous friends about the institution's substandard performance.

While building relationships as though they were meant to last makes abundant business sense and should be one of the fundamental goals of any communication program, it often isn't. Again, one must ask, why?

Second: Communication Programs Need to Be Where the Donor and Customer Are

Why aren't more organizations in tune with the long-term benefits of maximizing donor and customer longevity? The simple answer may be that it is easier for some institutions to have blinders on and not see markets as they really are than to see them clearly. Markets can be fractious and may not agree with where an organization is going or appreciate the emotional quality and urgency of the organization's causal decision-making. Marketplace opinions may also be counter to the wisdom emanating from an institution, which can be especially crucial and difficult when these opinions differ from those of the organizations that have enjoyed a degree of stakeholder and causal success. In such cases, it is often emotionally easier for an organization to take markets for granted than to spend time trying to understand their nuances, especially if stakeholder opinions and values are shifting. As a consequence, ignoring a market can lead to—or in some cases may be the result of— institutional arrogance. An agency may feel that it is leading the stakeholders and is uniquely in a position to know more than they.

The repercussions of such tactical moves are often severe. First, donors and customers must have access to an agency they are interested in the way they want to, any time of the day, and from any place they want to. In addition, ignoring the need to speak to stakeholders about the benefits of their involvement, refusing to give them information in a way that they can recognize, and not speaking to them of mutually held values creates consumer immobility and inaction. This inertia becomes a restraint to successfully creating a relational focus and intensity.

A nonprofit communication program should instead take the strategic steps of being open-minded about the causal markets stakeholders are interested in and include them as arbiters of what is or is not acceptable. These actions not only make sense causally and lead to leadership and excellence within an agency's communication programs, they also lead to marketplace truths that may not necessarily be confirmed by the firm's preexisting notions. Given the volume of messages individuals are exposed to (some estimate between 500–1800 separate messages per day), organizations cannot afford to communicate just for communication's sake. Agency communication programs must be structured so that they can be received and acted on by stakeholders. In addition, good communication programs must become an impetus to organizational democracy, something many donors demand today. Building strong, emotional attachments between stakeholder and agency allows donors, customers, and volunteers to dig deep in good times as well as in times of agency emergencies. In addition, recipients of good communication programs often become multicause or multibrand users and buyers within an agency if it is so set up. Further, they encourage those closest to them to become actively involved in the same projects they are involved in.

Conscientiously designed communication programs function as though everyone's contribution is important and considered, and they consequently aim to keep the stakeholder/organization relationships intact as long as possible. Embracing this attitude, organizational media spend less time "telling" and more time "guiding." The stakeholder macrocosm is a complex organism filled with dozens of competing claims on an individual's heart, loyalty, time, and pocketbook. Any agency must ask in regard to its communication program, "What will it take to break through this clutter and establish the trust and credibility we must have to survive relationally long term?" Will it take more brochures? An Internet presence? A team of field representatives? More public relations?

Third: It's about Them and Not You

Charles Handy suggests that, "Any business that concentrates on its internal mechanisms more than on customers is, ultimately, a bad business."[5] In other words, your communication program must first be about "them" before it is about "you." In trying to make it difficult for your audience to defect to another cause or proposition, you must know your audience to be able to tell them stories that interest them. An agency that fails to do this typically spends more time talking about itself rather than those that enable the causal work to continue. When an institution becomes centered on causal product within its communication media, it often becomes positioned by stakeholders against similar programs run by other agencies. Seeing nothing unique that ties the organization to their personal value set, they can feel the cause is just one more "me-to" communication filled with marketing hype. Similarly, by not working hard to be distinctive, the agency assumes that a far broader audience than is realistic will support its cause. Trying to appeal to everyone often results in appealing to very few, as the agency becomes too vague and abstract in its promotional media.

Much has been made in this text about knowing your audience. The reasons are simple. Given both the ease of starting a nonprofit organization in the United States and the widespread need that exists in our world, it is easy to imagine a society in which the supply of donative dollars in some stakeholder sectors simply cannot keep up with the volume of requests. Many more causal competitors are chasing the same dollars, which puts the stakeholder in the driver's seat. Quite frankly, most nonprofit organizations operate as though they don't know their audience. Stakeholders are not often made to feel "inside" the organization, nor are the initiatives stakeholders have expressed interest in written about. Help lines, information lines, or web sites, set up specifically for donors, volunteers, and customers may be hard to find and seem nonexistent. Valuable newsletter, webzines, and brochure column inches may also be filled with profiles of agency bureaucrats, talking about their interests but not necessarily those of concern to stakeholders.

What is required in knowing your audience is an organizational culture and attitude that can listen to many voices simultaneously, run its operations purposefully, and not fold in on itself. This can be extremely difficult operationally, because not all stakeholder opinions, goals, and aspirations align themselves with an institution's. However, individuals supporting organizations are not simply empty vessels waiting to have the faucet of agency communication turned on in order to flow into them. They also have feelings, values, and opinions. Consequently, an appreciation must be learned for the times when a stakeholder's opinion differs from the agency's. This gracious attitude must stem from a willingness not to let organizational fear preclude outside input as well as a desire to be as collaborative as possible with many different stakeholders in order to jointly provide service for individuals in need of help.

However, some organizational leaders do not feel they have the time for this type of listening effort, suggesting that the demands on their time are already too severe. They choose to operate on a daily basis rather than spend time worrying about whether there is alignment between agency and stakeholder. Although this attitude is not uncommon, there is reason to be cautious in running any type of closed operation. In a highly competitive universe, it is principally the organizations that can command support from many different stakeholder groups by being seen as credible that will succeed in the nonprofit marketplace. To achieve this level of trust and credibility requires an organization's leaders to decide that they are going to discover the goals, values, aims, and aspirations of key stakeholders and try to relate them to their organization and vice versa. Truth-telling on both sides is needed, as is the need for an organization to know exactly what it hopes to accomplish and how. Only then can an institution truly ask for involvement and support. As trite as this might sound, being concerned about and listening to others is an organizational trait that is needed if an agency's leadership hopes to have as many supporters as possible for its efforts. Individuals must believe an organization's leadership has their interests at heart before they will be willing to follow in pursuit of large, critical goals.

Fourth: Who Are You and What Is Your Agency "Voice"?

Before a strategy can be conceived or brochures written, an organization must decide what it wants to sound like to its stakeholders and what symbol and appearance it wants to assume in the reader's or listener's mind. This is not solely about dispensing information; rather, it is about the values an agency will exhibit in its communication and how it wishes to differentiate itself from the pack. In essence, this is a decision to move from a laissez-faire approach in communicating to one that has a strategic focus.

No one is more important to this process than the chief executive officer. During the past few years the role of the CEO has increased in importance in this task, with some leaders acting in effect as the senior marketing communications officer of their institutions alongside their CEO role. Assuming this psychological and pragmatic responsibility could not be more timely than it is right now, inasmuch as it is also increasingly the job of the senior spokesperson to articulate a public vision for the organization and to become its embodiment and voice. For example, when asked how much time he spends communicating (with internal and external stakeholders), Dell's Kevin Rollins replied, "Can you go above 100%?"[6]

To be competitive, an agency and its spokespersons need to have a dominant characteristic that is both consistent in its approach and appeals to groups of consumers, donors, customers, or volunteers. This character image must be as concrete as possible while triggering strong feelings. The stronger the character and the more stable the image an organization projects and the more it avoids competitive sameness, the more likely it will serve as a lightning rod to help attract individuals to the values and culture it inhabits.

An organization's character can be seen as interventionist, fun, caring, thoughtful, cutting edge, ministerial, or consumer friendly. Many profit and nonprofit annual reports often display their dominant character image on the front cover of their report. A recent search of some reports for a client showed a cross on one, a young orphan child smiling and eating on another, a similarly looking group of young people all dressed in black on still another, and a cover featuring the agency's name in lowercase type. There are many options and voices available to an organization. If for example, an agency's brand is built on the personality of being thoughtful, its communication program's voice should be seen as intelligent, caring, and collaborative, asking important questions and finding answers while appearing to be genuine. Professor Dallas Willard gives a current example of "voice." "In many churches today the services have divided into 'traditional' and 'contemporary,' primarily over imagery and the feelings attached therein. The guitar and pipe organ are no longer just musical instruments, they are powerful symbols."[7]

Fifth: Communication Must Be Integrated

Creating a strong donor, customer, or volunteer experience is one of the great accomplishments in a nonprofit organization's life and an important by-product of a good communication program. This experience is typically cemented through a bundled series of occurrences that the stakeholder has with the organization, not solely through a single communication medium or contact with one employee. Stakeholders listen to an organization visually, multidimensionally, in abstract ways, and through normative text and audio outlets.

An example of this type of bundled listening is that of an organization that had a great donor magazine that garnered a lot of positive feedback. However, the emotional impact of this communication piece with one stakeholder was muted when the organization's receipting program, which manifested a tendency to credit gifts erroneously and routinely misspell donors' names, sent a receipt with errors on it to the stakeholder in question. Individuals gain their impression of an organization through various media; in the case of this donor, there were both good and bad impressions along what is popularly referred to as "the thousand points of donor contact."

Every part of an organization communicates meaning and becomes a part of a stakeholder's bank of impressions. This includes all the contact elements that make up an agency's stakeholder communication plan along with items that may not have been intended as communication vehicles, such as how an agency's programs are run or designed. Regardless of purpose, these items contribute to the overall impression an individual forms of an organization.

REAL-WORLD EXAMPLES

I had the privilege of working with a humanitarian group that was sending workers into economically troubled spots in the third world. The workers—or "emissaries"—that were being sent were a fine group of men and women, willing to give two years of their lives on behalf of individuals living in countries with few resources. Given the sending group's integrity, interpersonal competencies, and communication abilities, I privately thought that the need for donor support for this agency would easily be subscribed. Unfortunately, the primary piece of promotional literature for the organization was a two-color brochure printed on cheap stock, featuring a picture of the organization's founder and a lengthy version of its credo. Nowhere within the brochure were there pictures of those who were going to be helped by the organization's efforts nor was there a description of the benefits a stakeholder would receive by being a part of this humanitarian effort.*

*From the personal files of Barry McLeish.

The promotional piece broke character with the rest of the personality of the organization. Copy, logo, presentation, and design mitigated against the importance of the humanitarian task and the earnestness of the those going overseas. The emotional touchpoints a stakeholder might have had with this promotional piece and the cause it represented were not integrated with an appropriate description of who the men and women being sent were, what they represented, and what they wanted to provide through their service. Three problems occur simultaneously with a reader—or listener for that fact—when their expectations are not met with the realizations of what is communicated:

1. In this instance, the errant communication piece sold a product and vision that was different from what the young emissaries represented. There was little connection between the two and, hence, no leverage.

2. Often designed for large, mass-market segments of people, nonprofit communication is frequently designed, written, and spoken in as general terms as possible. The idea that effective discourse habitually has to be written to an "audience of one" is forgotten. With language written or spoken in an imprecise manner, no emotional connection is created for the reader. Instead, the name of virtually any competitive cause undertaking a similar mission can be substituted within the communication for the organization's name with hardly any meaning being lost to the reader or listener.

3. Consequently, in this example the brand's compelling identity in light of its intervention into parts of the world that are at risk was not communicated or presented in its promotional efforts in a way that the audiences could see and experience it.

Given the goal of retaining donors, customers, and volunteers for longer periods of time, perhaps it is not too difficult to surmise that the overall goal of an effective communication program ought to be as much a matter of keeping stakeholders involved emotionally in the organization as of selling them on giving, volunteering, or buying again. Capturing the attention of these collaborative partners becomes a critical pursuit, as does staying with them emotionally until they become relational partners. As organizational communication tools have become increasingly interactive, this goal has also become increasingly achievable. Treating market segments as smaller and more precise allows nonprofit communication, marketing, and development managers to speak of goals that can include drawing stakeholders into deeper, more fulfilling relationships with the agency, while maintaining the give and take of a flowing relational tapestry. Therefore, the goal of an integrated communication program should be that of developing progressively deeper attachments whereby both parties—stakeholder and agency—realize increased levels of satisfaction based on collaborative camaraderie and mutual value achievement.

To achieve this goal, any agency today has to look at its stakeholders' lifestyle and the values they embody to be in alignment with what they hope and desire for the organization. This is often achieved through the creation of a cultural tapestry, and its creation is the subject of Chapter 8.

▨ NOTES

1. Iacobucci, Dawn and Bobby Calder, eds., Kellogg on Integrated Marketing (New York: John Wiley & Sons, 2003), p. xvi.
2. From the personal files of Barry McLeish.
3. Handy, Charles, The Hungry Spirit (New York: Broadway Books, 1998), p. 52.
4. Clancy, Kevin J. and Robert S. Shulman, The Marketing Revolution (New York: HarperBusiness, 1991), p. 237.
5. Ibid., Handy, p. 10.

6. As quoted in Argenti, Paul A., Robert A. Howell, and Karen A. Beck, "The Strategic Communication Imperative," MIT Sloan Management Review, vol. 46, no.3, Spring 2005, p. 88.

7. Willard, Dallas, Renovation of the Heart (Colorado Springs: NAVPRESS, 2002), p. 99.

CHAPTER 8

The Fifth Issue: Creating the Cultural Tapestry

When the seminar leader noted that, "The world is more complex today than yesterday," her observation during my time at a training event proved to be the understatement of the week. With our competitive culture moving inextricably toward complexity and chaos, much of the nonprofit world no longer seems to be the composed plane it once was. Where nonprofit organizations once seemingly operated in calm and secure spaces, seldom moving out of equilibrium with their surroundings and economies, today many are overstretched and at the peak of their delivery capabilities. The changes they are encountering is as Igor Ansoff suggested in his *New Corporate Strategy*, discontinuous, neither predictive nor in keeping with the history of events most institutions have encountered in their past. And with nonprofit organizational change now being both continuous and ingrained, hypercompetition, misalignment, a lack of management resolve, confusion, and disorganization are common themes running through many agencies.

Nonprofit stakeholders are also experiencing their own personal form of discontinuity. As the balance of power and influence shifts from agency to stakeholder, consumers are struggling to create philanthropic experiences that are uniquely suited to their own

individual needs and tastes. Daniel Yankelovich gave a foreshadow-
ing of this in *New Rules: Searching for Self-fulfillment in a World Turned
Upside Down*, in which he suggested that individuals were looking
for more sacred and intrinsic benefits in their work rather than
viewing it as a means to an end. The same thing could be said about
how people are involved philanthropically today. Overwhelmed by
both the number of causal choices they face and the number of
causal messages aimed at them, men and women are searching for
institutions they perceive will bring value to them personally along
with new relationships, networks, and empowerment. Marc Gobe,
in his book *Citizen Brand*, suggests that individuals, "want to
emotionally vibrate together."[1]

As a consequence of these forces, new notions such as "interactive
communities," "causal networks," "hyperaggressive environments,"
and "continuous causal innovation" describe and redefine the
world in which nonprofit institutions now operate. The need and
expectation among some stakeholder audiences of mutual agency
collaboration and the tactical necessity institutions have to build
long-lasting relationships with many different types of clientele
contribute to this complexity. With it comes reason to believe also
that the clangor of third-sector organizational perplexity can only
get louder.

Peter Drucker, in *The New Realities*, suggests that throughout
Western history sharp transformations have occurred that he calls
"divide(s)." Many agencies in the nonprofit world are experiencing
such a divide as they seek to rearrange themselves, their operating
structures, and the way they conduct business in pursuit of their
causal goals. What is driving these changes?

At stake is nothing less than the success of organizations in
reaching their missional goals. Finding that it is impossible to have
all the necessary expertise, accumulated resources, and personnel
competencies residing in-house, progressive agencies are increasingly looking for ways to develop causal alliances or networks
outside their institutional borders. With the goal of developing new

capacities while keeping costs in line, many nonprofits are seeking collaborative partnerships with individuals or groups who have expertise in areas of concern and assistance to an agency. In addition, these "new voices" are also helping agencies create fresh mental maps in their pursuit of causal goals at a time when habitual ways of seeing the world are no longer useful, given the unfamiliar emerging realities.

Not all in the nonprofit world concur on the need to take these actions. Although many executives agree that there are qualitative differences in the changes they are now seeing in the present decade as opposed to the preceding one, other agency leaders have responded to these situations by doing little or nothing about them or have instead applied old solutions to new problems. Others, however, believing that futurist John Naisbitt is correct when he suggests the best way to see the future is to understand what is happening now, realize that the critical organizational question for them is, "How can our institution effectively achieve its goals successfully in a hypercompetitive milieu?"

Understanding the Relationship between Stakeholder Values and Strategy

To compete successfully often requires an agency to move from what is "known" operationally to what is "unknown." Advancing from a passive organizational stance to one that is opportunistic may lead some institutions to perceive the need to develop new operational principles that affect their strategy, culture, and infrastructure.

For example, in many nonprofit agencies competition is thought to be a "known" arena and is viewed operationally as a fixed set of activities whose end goal is to figure out how to outplay or outperform those the agency competes with. In situations where the causal industry is established and the methods by which work is accomplished are relatively defined or understood by all players, an institution may undertake such a competitive strategy and achieve moderate success. If, for example, an agency finds its stakeholder environment to be comparatively stable and composed principally of an aging donor base that is relatively passive and satisfied, outperforming competitors through competitive selling of its features and benefits may be an appropriate strategy.

However, in more discontinuous environments, this strategy would most likely be the wrong choice. Upon finding itself in such surroundings, an agency must first assess its competitive environment and then determine what strategic paradigms it can possibly employ. In doing so the agency has a better chance of rising above normal competitive responses and to begin to change the causal playing field to suit its own purposes. For example, in a fairly turbulent, hyper-competitive environment, with donor and volunteer constituencies exercising their own authority and power while showing little institutional loyalty, an agency may want to change its competitive focus. Moving away from the tactical status quo of trying to "outdo each other" (employed by most competitors), an institution could focus on the relationships occurring between the agency and its stakeholders, the purpose behind these relationships, and the choice of strategy it chooses to enact. Because many nonprofit organizations fail to acknowledge the emotional and pragmatic link between a stakeholder's personal values and the strategy it employs, agencies can gain insights by seeing not only the intertwining of the values exhibited by target markets, but the level of competition and the strategy challengers are employing. Having moved away from a "me too" sense of strategy, an institution is now in a position to know both the rules of the playing field and the ingredients needed to better tailor its strategy to the surrounding environment.

Tailoring an organization's response to its environment allows it a better chance to establish strategic ascendancy by introducing new benchmarks of success, helpful whether one is challenging the status quo organizationally, trying to introduce a new way of operating, or simply asking stakeholders, "Is there a way to create a different future together?" Is there a benchmark of success that is more valuable to stakeholder and organization alike? Yes, there is indeed a superior form of collaborative value creation, designed by both of them with both of them in mind.

The Need to Create Collaboration across Communities

Environmental and stakeholder turbulence should be a signal to third-sector agencies. Unfortunately, it often isn't. What is the turbulence a signal of? Nonprofit institutions are finding that in the eyes of many stakeholders, being a good organization is not enough. Stakeholders are looking for a relevancy and emotional attachment in those agencies they support. They want to love, identify with, and be connected with causes that mirror the values they hold.

Therefore, looking at the urgency of reengineering endeavors across a broad range of systems and activities, as opposed to the notion of a single, silver bullet, cutting-edge nonprofit leaders are examining and reshaping virtually everything about their organizations to reflect stakeholder sentiments and the impermanence of the times. This type of corporate transience is leading many to see the need for a different type of nonprofit agency, one that is open to building new alliances based on stakeholder emotional commitments and collaboration. The desired outcome is the integration of various existing donor, volunteer, customer, and expert subcultures with expertise that is either lacking within an institution or is not in plentiful supply.

With supply exceeding demand in some donative markets, it is not unusual to find causal organizations that are unable to sustain their own performance goals. Many institutions in this predicament need to augment their strategic presence by doing something different tactically. For some of them, "doing something different" means changing from a relatively closed agency to becoming a highly networked operational organization that can work with people possessing different sets of competencies and skills with whom alliances can be formed. Together, their purposive behavior is directed at achieving the end goal for which the nonprofit was created.

With stakeholder autonomy now the new marketplace currency, agencies are increasingly being forced to become both flexible and collaborative in their outlook. The reasons for this are simple. "Tough times are the norm," says author and lecturer Michael Hammer.[2] The average stakeholder is now exposed to somewhere between 2,000 to 4,000 advertising messages per day through all types of media, with many messages alarmingly intrusive and seemingly out of control. With deep-rooted anger about being subjected to appeal and advertising clutter, stakeholders are increasingly looking at products and causal agencies that promise to enhance their donative experience rather than detract from it. In doing so, most want to create a different future together with the organization(s) they are interested in.

As suggested, however, not all agencies have taken this veiled warning to heart. For example, countless nonprofit texts and seminars tell organizations to focus on—and listen to—the consumer; so much so that the notion has practically become a third-sector platitude. However, as the following story suggests, too few institutions have yet to change their practices.

REAL-WORLD EXAMPLES

I have a close friend whose daughter wanted to spend one year in Asia with a well-known nonprofit organization helping men and women less fortunate than she. Having applied to the agency and been accepted, she had to first raise $18,000 to help defray her expenses overseas. She then received some comprehensive orientation and training for her Asian assignment over a period of months from the sponsoring organization. Finally, she had to get physically and psychologically tested before she left for her assignment. In the process of trying to get a question answered regarding his daughter's terms of service, her father called the sponsoring agency and asked to speak to the person coordinating her assignment. He was told the gentleman in charge was out of the office for one week. Feeling the issue was important he then asked for the gentleman's cell phone number in order to leave a message and was informed this number was not given out publicly. Could he speak to the gentleman's assistant? the father then asked. The assistant was sick and away from her desk. My friend then asked to speak to the next person in charge and was informed that apart from the two individuals previously sought after, no one else in the office was capable of answering his question. Feeling a little concerned about entrusting his daughter to an organization while still having questions that needed resolution, he then asked for the supervisor's e-mail address and sent him a message outlining his questions and concerns. Somewhat reluctantly, the father of the young woman also left a voice mail message on the gentleman's office answering system and finally got a call back four days later.

Perhaps this story is not typical (though it seems every nonprofit seminar and text speaks of similar examples). In the good old days, this may have been acceptable organizational behavior especially in the light of stakeholders who were often passive, toed the organizational line, and inconspicuously waited for agencies to respond to their concerns in the agency's own good time. It seems harsh words were rarely spoken between institutions and the customers and donors involved with them.

Instead, look at the outcomes in this unfortunate example:

- The quality of the interaction between the father and agency was tainted; it imprinted their mutual experience from the beginning and lessened the chance of future collaboration between the two parties.

- The nonprofit agency inadvertently restricted the flow of information to the stakeholder, who was simply looking for additional data in order to feel that his decision was a correct one, causing suspicion between the two.

- Stakeholder scrutiny—an important part of the decision-making apparatus—had limits put on it where none should have existed.

Issue Five: Creating the Cultural Tapestry

Stakeholders have obviously turned up the heat considerably. Spurred by both their new-found marketplace power as well as by the large numbers of nonprofit organizations that are now engaged in similar causal behaviors—thereby creating situations of causal and organizational parity—stakeholders have not only begun to change the rules of the game, but in some cases, to change the game as well. After having been ignored by a handful of agencies for years and now more willing to push their own causal agendas with the purpose of creating individualized value, some stakeholders—angered by decades of nonprofit corporate inattention—view agencies as being in their employ, as opposed to the dominant notion in some of these organizations that just the opposite is true. According to Lewis P. Carbone, founder of Experience Engineering Inc., consumers, "have become unpredictable free agents: increasingly disappointed, disgruntled, devalued, and ultimately disloyal."[3]

With the ability to uncover access to intelligence unavailable in previous times along with countless networking opportunities, nonprofit stakeholders are also able to examine causal services side-by-side on an unprecedented scale. Notes Larry Johnston, president and chief executive officer of the consulting group McConkey/ Johnston International, "Not only are they no longer afraid to voice their own opinions, stakeholders have created a new day for nonprofit organizations and their directors, whether they like it or not."[4]

It's obvious that some nonprofit directors don't like it. Whether viewed as stakeholder extremism or merely as a distraction from the proper workings of their organizations, it is clear that a smattering of nonprofit executives regard listening to stakeholders to the point of sometimes adopting their ideas as a waste of time, or at least a nuisance that must be tolerated. The president of a large international relief agency confessed, "Though I am trying to listen a lot more than ever before to the individuals in my constituencies, the ideas and comments I tend to get are often not in keeping with where I want to go personally, nor in how I want to attack both our programming needs and leverage their financial gifts and that of their friends."[5]

Though this attitude may be warranted in some instances, persisting in it over time allows directors to insulate themselves further and further from their agency's supporters and possible collaborators. The end result of an institutional leadership team's closing itself off from outside influences can mean hampering impending developments and abridging innovation that often comes as a direct result of this type of collaboration, not to mention the endless possibilities that can come from an open attitude toward the future as opposed to a closed one.

Unfortunately, attempting to shelter oneself from the outside world is a strategy that comes from trying to control future events while artificially placing a value on those the nonprofit agency is collaborating with. Leadership teams that try to eliminate outside stakeholder influences along with the customary obscurity and vagueness present in any organization that operates with an eye to the future, soon find this to be a futile enterprise. However, when this type of culture and cognitive control is imposed by senior management onto an agency's inner workings, it only helps ensure that new perspectives and innovative behaviors that could arise through new information and knowledge, co-creation, and collaboration are limited. While new ideas and innovation may still emerge within groups that close themselves off, they often do so in a way that is not in keeping with creating the marketplace advantages that come from meeting new stakeholder values. In addition, the ideas and innovation that are produced may arrive too late to be competitively helpful. Consequently, the flow of outside information, effectively cut off because of the culture management imposes, leads increasingly to institutions that experience hardships in hypercompetitive futures. Is there a way for such hardships to be avoided? Yes, and it involves these three critical issues:

1. There is a need for third-sector organizations to approach collaborative relationships in a new way.

2. Organizations must decide how they want to compete in the future, and whether they want to involve possible collaborators or not. They must also consider the effect this decision might have on how they are evolving.

3. Issues of organizational culture and identity must be decided in order to embrace possible collaborators.

First: The Need for a New Organizational Tapestry

There are few more difficult issues for some leaders in the nonprofit management ranks to accept than the new sense that organizational leadership must become increasingly dynamic and collaborative in order to succeed. Part of this dilemma stems from an emerging moral contract with stakeholders that says nonprofit organizations must do more than take resources from them; instead, they must also mutually create value with the stakeholder in a shared destiny. Authors and consultants William Belgard and Steven Rayner, in their book *Shaping the Future*, call this situation "the emerging megadigm,"—their word for the profound changes that have occurred in customer expectations that managers cannot ignore.[6] Not only are the world views of nonprofit managers changing as a result of this "megadigm" but given that agencies are increasingly encountering unplanned and rapidly changing circumstances, management continuously needs to decide how it will adapt to these unsettling conditions.

As suggested, the first tendency for many leaders in the face of unsettling conditions is to try and enact control systems. Though still a dominant and operational concept in hundreds of nonprofit agencies, the concept of tight-fisted control as an operating norm is fast becoming outdated, particularly as nonprofit macrocosms experience a profound sense of audience fragmentation across all types of media and causal platforms.

Much of what is happening in and to the nonprofit environment simply cannot be predicted. Perhaps this is fortunate. Given both the causal needs of this world and the elaborate responses many organizations have erected to meet these exigencies, there is a necessity for some institutions to evolve and remain open to new ways of doing things, even if conditions force them into it. Without such pressure and the infusion of new knowledge, the operational stance that many agencies currently hold to, will simply not meet the demands placed upon them and the objectives the agencies hold to unless they are adapted and renewed.

REAL-WORLD EXAMPLES

For example, is there an issue that elicits more profound emotional response within nonprofit agencies than asking for support, financial or otherwise? This is extremely unfortunate. When they are recognized for the benefit done on behalf of mankind, correctly managed nonprofit agencies can become social and economic institutions for incredible good. In spite of the abundance of charity generated in this country, some third-sector organizations suffer from a perplexing community vacillation regarding both their need and worthiness because of the style and methodology they employ in their fund-raising practices. Typically, agencies who find themselves in these situations go about their fund-raising without engaging the public in a collaborative and face-to-face, individualistic manner. Instead, they often rely solely on mass advertising efforts, crying "emergency" and "urgency" as much as they dare, utilizing strategies that view the donor, customer, and volunteer relationship as expendable. Supported routinely and heavily by a relative few, they are concurrently held in deep suspicion by others.

Stakeholders of course, are right to hold some nonprofit organizations and their leaders suspect. The fault, however, does not typically lie in the worthiness of these institutions or the level of benevolence generated by them as much as in how agency leaders manage their affairs, particularly in relation to those who support them. In these business practices (frequently closed to outside inspection), agency convention and habit has caused nonprofit leaders to subvert their own significance. Why?

First, the most critical of these practices is the failure of leadership to recognize that many of today's and tomorrow's donors are looking for more in their relationship with the agencies they are interested in than they currently receive from them. Most nonprofit establishments do an excellent job at being fiscally minded and conscientious in their business dealings. In addition, many of these same agencies are thoroughly professional in their fund-raising practices and operating efficiencies. What is happening, tactically speaking, is that while organizations are becoming experts at controlling their empires fiscally and taking or appropriating value from existing stakeholder friends through donations, purchases, and volunteerism, they have concurrently done a poorer job at giving value back to these same stakeholders. This is not just a tragedy but an immense marketing error as well. Amidst the hypercompetitive and parity markets many causes are a part of, as well as the changes new technology and programmatic innovation brings, shared value creation in a relationship of mutual destinies may be one of the most critical marketing defenses nonprofit organizations can marshal today.

However, there is a second even more critical reason why social-sector institutions should create value-added partnerships. Complementary, collaborative partnerships offer a competitive advantage in the hypercompetitive world of parity causes. Individuals that have successful transactions with an agency often want to do more on its behalf. Many want to give back more than money. For some, this means volunteering to perform a low-level task. Others, however, may be looking for something different. For example, when the invitation comes to an individual from an agency to explicitly give back by co-constructing a future built on trust and corresponding values with the same group the individual supports, this presents an opportunity for personal identification that typically does not come to most supporting nonprofit work. It moves the relationship with a stakeholder from a simple transaction where a perfunctory receipt and "thank you" are transmitted to a higher level of intimacy. This goes beyond giving one's advice through an anonymous survey or joining a "President's Association" filled with inane premiums, to enabling one's personal values to be jointly transacted along with that of an agency's, becoming jointly a provider of value solutions.

What does "giving back" look like? Unfortunately, it is often categorized and limited by institutions to mean giving back more money or giving back advice that ultimately goes unheeded. Too seldom do the leaders of a cause think of their thankful constituents as a means to create not only knowledge that can lead to new efficiencies and innovation within the agency's operating practices but also donor satisfaction and tenure. Perhaps this is because directors often fear they may lose their positional power or control through such an alliance. This may be a real fear in some cases, but the view is shortsighted. The presence today of causal hypercompetition puts a premium on joint value creation and new knowledge.

Both of these expressions lead to continuous expertise expansion within an agency. Further, individuals with competencies valuable to an agency often utilize this capability on behalf of the institution gratis and, in the process, become a catalyst for agency differentiation and tenure. The net effect is that the individual and organization become engaged together with the entire structure benefiting. By being able to access new competencies outside an organization and by bringing those competencies inside, a nonprofit agency creates a learning environment that is not dependent on itself, limited to its own resources, or tied to a particular social infrastructure. What's more, inherent in an institution's pursuit of individuals providing collaborative assistance and creating new causal knowledge is the basis for causal differentiation, competitive advantage, and service innovation.

Access, mutual trust, reciprocity, and a clear understanding of the need and objective allowed the events in the following example to happen and empowered both directors and collaborators alike.

REAL-WORLD EXAMPLES

A group of agency donors including two engineers, an earth-moving equipment operator, a couple of building trade professionals, and some friends took it upon themselves to design, excavate, and build a ski and tubing hill for a cause involving young people. They got involved in the project because the agency director initiated a conversation with one of them, shared his dream for such a structure, and asked for advice for how to go about making it a reality. Excited by the openness of the director in his need for help, the fellow brought into the conversation suggested he convene a task force made up of some agency donors and personal friends on behalf of the project. The project captured the imagination of many of the organization's supporters, and it was built and opened 18 months later.

Another institution, facing its second year of decline, empowered a donor the director knew to be an advertising agency copywriter to provide any advice she could about how it should be portrayed in print and solicitations. The director opened herself up and showed the copywriter the private results of what was working and what was not. The young writer went back to her employer, consulted the staff on a volunteer basis as to their ideas. and was able to implement them within the nonprofit group. Later, she got her agency involved in some pro bono work, helping to bring about an increase in community participation along with more donations to the cause.

Still another nonprofit organization—a museum—had its exhibit area refurbished and paid for by volunteers who had done the same with another institution. Upon hearing of this, the director inquired as to the volunteers' availability to help the agency he headed. They agreed to help, and in fact, these volunteers continued to find and procure exhibits for the new museum partner for many years. Focusing on their technical competence, the director created an environment where their collaboration resulted in new learning for the institution.

In each situation stakeholders were entrusted with tasks that enabled them to see themselves as a part of the larger value-adding activities that had a strategic part to play within the agencies they cared about. A shared vision and opportunity, partnership, and a real need enabled mutual endeavors and alliances to take place. Achieving the causal goals through the agency added value to both cause and stakeholder. Though having a clear reason to do the projects and doing them together were important, the long-lasting relationships that were built and cemented were even more so.

How can an agency adapt and renew itself to achieve mutual value creation while being open to the other benefits that a tapestry of support can bring to it? This can be accomplished through some surprisingly pragmatic steps.

Second: Know What Your Organization Is Becoming

Competitive discontinuities—whether better-informed stake-holders, shorter causal product life cycles, the battle between old and new technology advocates, or the greater transparency required of nonprofit organizations—demand changes in how institutions operate. Surprisingly, many agencies simply do not know who they have become in light of these social and environmental changes, why they operate as they do, and what makes them unique. If they had a firmer grasp of these issues, the idea of developing new capabilities with others around the notions of trust, individual competency, and reciprocity might not be perceived as problematic as it generally is.

To know what your organization is becoming, you first must know where it is presently. Many institutional leaders don't know how to answer this question. For example, in countless interviews across many causal agency types, consistent answers by institutional leaders or leadership teams to the following questions are often the exception and not the norm.

- What is the organization's vision and aim?
- What makes it different and vital from others doing the same work?
- What human values is the agency fulfilling within stake-holders?
- What is the organization accomplishing of a permanent nature?

The inability of some leadership teams to respond coherently to these questions may help explain why some leaders and their staff both worry inordinately about how their organizational content is viewed by various stakeholder audiences. In the process of worrying, they try to control how and when it is observed and who then is allowed access to the group. Inopportunely, trying to maintain this type of control while concurrently endeavoring to adapt to the needs of an agency's consumers results in conflicting departmental beliefs and, often enough, in strategic institutional schizophrenia.

The notion of "knowing what you are becoming" organizationally is important for four primary reasons:

1. As mentioned in an earlier chapter 7, we live in an over-communicated society where most nonprofit institutions are trying to communicate more vigorously while simultaneously seeking someone to listen to them. The difficulties this ultimately represents to the average organization are immense and complicated, especially in trying to convey one's identity to a variety of audiences. Because of the problems associated with this difficult task, some nonprofit agencies end up either trying to mimic other institutions, focusing on the other and what they are providing to the marketplace, or presenting a falsified or "fabricated" image of what they would like the public to believe they are—but really are not—in order to appeal to as large an audience as possible.

2. The second reason that knowing where you are going organizationally is important is the immense pressure that is on nonprofit agencies to be distinctive. With the notion of established nonprofit agency crowdedness and congruity as commonplace as it is now, when one institution causally innovates in the field it becomes the new standard by which every other agency in its causal field is measured almost immediately. In the subsequent race to catch up, some philanthropic fields are filled with "me-too" causal products that do little to differentiate themselves from one another. The consequence of this lack of action typically is an underfunded cause that struggles for survival.

3. Market research has also contributed to this causal sameness in some heavily solicited and marketed customer fields, creating

a type of institutional congruity with respect to different types of donor and customer promotion, and encouraging similar marketing and fundraising approaches to audiences that, in turn, garner comparable response rates. For some organizations caught in this spiral, consumer research has often caused nonprofit groups to proliferate their causal programs, trying to become "all things to all people." The net return to an organization that adopts such a strategy may be initially perceived as trendy and popular, though not necessarily filled with substantial programming that over time garners substantial results.

4. Analogous technologies embraced by nonprofit agencies have also allowed and even propelled a type of organizational and causal product sameness to continue and prosper. Across agencies, administrative and strategy teams armed with similar computer models and tools have often successfully created commensurate marketing and fund-raising tactics, mirroring each other to donors and customers. This particularly happens in the donor acquisition arena, with nonprofit marketing departments spreading as broad a net as possible by employing similar prospecting, procurement, and financial models.

Are there resolutions for these dilemmas? Yes, and part of the answer—and hence a good part of an organization's future—may lie with how institutions create new information and, how they create continuous value for their stakeholders. At the most basic level, this is an issue of how a nonprofit organization sets up its operational culture. Without a culture that allows many current operations to habitually be opened up to the new emerging realities stakeholders are bringing with them, managers become doomed to being both protective of the ways in which they now operate and tied to the ways they operated in the past.

Third: Questions of Organizational Personality and Identity Must Precede More Popular Discussions of Brand and Image

With the emergence of lifestyle marketing as one of the givens in advertising and fundraising strategies, it is only natural that branding has become one of the more popular topics among nonprofit leaders. It is hard to deny branding's importance, especially when a stakeholder supports a nonprofit organization entrenched in its mission and feels a profound emotional connection to it within his or her heart. When it comes to implementing an actual brand strategy, most nonprofit tacticians do not understand how difficult it is to achieve, often relying primarily on visual expressions to achieve their branding effect through fancy brochures, logos, mass media, or symbols. To a lesser degree, events and verbal demonstrations are used to achieve similar branding objectives.

When asked about their branding goals, most development marketers specify variations of the following three:

1. To make their institution immediately recognizable in order to both manage its perception in stakeholders' eyes and to differentiate it from other causes, especially those within its causal industry.

2. To highlight an agency's strengths and reputation in the awareness and hearts of its stakeholders to make it easier for the organization's development team—or sales force—to attract necessary resources of all kinds to the cause.

3. To help stakeholders understand the strengths of an institution and recognize its high level of performance through which they can then feel a measure of pride in their association. (In for-profit circles this is called shareholder value, and it is equally important in nonprofit circles. The organizational goal of a strong brand identity is to build brand

equity through increased stakeholder recognition, loyalty, and awareness.)

There is a lot to be gained from a branding discussion, but what is typically not heard within the exciting discussion of logos, brochures, and the like is the idea that it is the inner substance of an organization that should become the embodiment of its outward expressions, not the other way around. Brands and causal behavior must be true to an institution's identity. What's more, branding's long-term success is heavily dependent on what an agency is saying through its development and marketing communication around the causal innovation on behalf of those it serves and those who support the cause. Without these necessary embodiments an organization stands in danger of becoming a "me-too" product.

How do nonprofit organizations typically communicate who they are to stakeholders so that they can, in turn, understand something of the identity of the organization they support or are involved in? The most common ways are through the following:

- **The physical presence of known agency personnel.** The people who work there often come to the mind of a stakeholder when the name of a specific organization is mentioned. Institutional representatives are concrete examples to customers, donors, and volunteers regarding the personality of an organization. When the demeanor or operational value of an agency representative is weak or individuals seem unsure of their loyalty or of the direction their sponsoring organization is taking, this confers to a stakeholder a picture of an organization not sure of who it is or where it is going. For example, in undertaking a branding project for an international organization, many discussions with overseas personnel indicated strong contrary feelings about the direction the organization was taking. When these views were expressed, the individuals holding them sounded disloyal and insubordinate to outsiders. This, in turn, created confusion in the minds of stakeholders about the future of the organization.

- **The infrastructure systems and services.** Systems and services show stakeholders the type of person an organization would be if it were living. In its support of the causal activity an organization engages in, systems and services become concrete representations of the agency in action to interested parties. In the earlier example of the young woman who wanted to serve overseas, the systems the organization employed to respond to her father's questions caused the agency to stumble badly and became emblematic to the father of the culture the organization reflected.

- **The transactional qualities.** The transactional qualities contribute directly to the strength or weakness of an exchange between a stakeholder and an organization and also serve as a barometer to the stakeholder of the way they should think about any future involvement with the institution. The critical psychological question typically asked by a stakeholder after a transaction is, "Did the exchange benefit or hinder the relationship between the agency and myself?" Does a stakeholder feel affirmed by his or her involvement or not? If, for example, people volunteer their time to undertake a particular task on behalf of an organization, on completion of the task did they feel appropriately thanked for their efforts? The emotions conjured up contribute to the strength or weakness of the transaction between both parties and help define how an individual feels as a result of being involved with the interchange.

- **The communication system.** The communication policies employed by an institution increasingly make clear to stakeholders whether an agency wants to listen to them and encourage them to become part of a community of supporters or merely wants to dispense words and images. Unfortunately, communication for many nonprofit agencies has come to mean mass-based advertising or solicitation, neither one particularly interested in listening to stakeholders, helping them solve their value problems, or building stakeholder good-will. Given that many mass-marketing campaigns are exhibiting symptoms of decline, the reflex reaction some institutions have of sending out more solicitations or making more calls in times of hypercompetition works against them. Traditional causal advertising messages are in some philanthropic industries so similar as to be ineffective. This impotency is further exasperated by the exponential growth of our media-driven culture and the burgeoning presence of stakeholder-friendly intelligence sources.

Many if not most donors, volunteers, and customers give to—or volunteer with—an organization they want to have some type of relationship with. Unfortunately, many institutions talk about building relationships with their constituents but too few do it, either lacking the tools, tactics, or will. In fact, the notion of relationship marketing has become mainstreamed in nonprofit circles and is now viewed as an operative tactic that agencies should use in their funding and marketing efforts. Though this type of marketing is defined operationally in many ways, when it is spoken of topically at development seminars or written about in nonprofit textbooks, it is often presented as a surefire and necessary tactic for raising money and maintaining donors and customers.

The essence of relationship marketing is usually introduced with the thought that people today are inundated with funding and purchasing requests. One way to break through the clamor of these requests is to befriend individual prospects one at a time or in small groupings, and over a period of contacts or visits, gain their trust. This often leads to their purchasing a product or donating a financial gift to the sponsoring organization. Usually presented as a linear and predictive system, the relationship in these scenarios enables the gift.

Clearly the institution profits in this enterprise, as does, ostensibly, the donor. What does the donor receive in this transaction? In interviewing hundreds of stakeholders, often not enough. Seldom given the same priority as agency needs in the relationship, the prospective collaborator is often left feeling the relationship stands for nothing and is little more than a tactic. It is seen as having no direction and going nowhere. Collaborative marketing can give an individual a chance at a radical relationship that transcends a transaction-only environment within an organization and can allow both parties to see their individual value goals fulfilled if

- The stakeholder sees the relationship as an alliance that has benefits tied to both parties. Both parties need access to the key strategic issues behind the alliance. It must be purpose driven. Relationships cannot be created in a vacuum.

- Collaborative meaning and knowledge must come out of the combined investigation of the issue, and this meaning and knowledge must become the fulcrum on which consensus is built, along with building, enhancing, and legitimizing the brand experience.

- Someone once said to me that marketers need to make customers feel safe and have no fear about their purchase. The same is most likely true of the philanthropic experience. Stakeholders need the stability that a good relationship affords and, in the context of the affiliation, they need to feel sought after and feel a sense of belongingness.

- Alliances need to be viewed as a renewable resource. To treat them solely as a short-term phenomenon is to ignore the effects and benefits of a long-term compact built as a true partnership.

Much of the nonprofit business zeitgeist on development, relationship marketing, and branding—as taught at so many nonprofit seminars—exaggerates the seller's contribution and minimizes the stakeholder's power. Typically, the implication is that everything grows out of the seller. Take the seller out of the equation and the donor is lost and confused. To ignore the stakeholder is to ignore the future of philanthropy.

NOTES

1. *Gobe, Marc,* Citizen Brand *(New York: Allworth Press, 2002), p. xxiii.*
2. *Hammer, Michael,* The Agenda *(New York: Crown Business, 2001), p. 3.*
3. *Carbone, Lewis P.,* Clued In *(New York: Financial Times Prentice Hall, 2004), as quoted by Charles Decker in* Fast Company, *December 2004, p. 97.*
4. *Larry Johnston in a seminar entitled,* Toward a Culture of Execution: Catalytic Mechanisms that Get Results *(at the McConkey/Johnston client conference in Colorado Springs, October 8–10, 2004).*
5. *From the personal files of Barry McLeish.*
6. *Belgard, William P. and Steven R. Rayner,* Shaping the Future *(New York: AMACOM, 2004), p. 2.*

REFERENCES

Ansoff, Igor, *New Corporate Strategy* (New York: John Wiley & Sons, 1988).

Drucker Peter, *The New Realities* (New York: HarperCollins, 1989).

Naisbitt, John, *Megatrends: Ten New Directions for Transforming Our Lives* (New York: Warner Books, 1982).

Yankelovich, Daniel, *New Rules: Searching for Self-fulfillment in a World Turned Upside Down* (New York: Random House, 1981).

Afterword

OPERATING AS IF THE FUTURE WERE UNSURE

A client who runs a large organization for young people and their families on the East coast has enjoyed amazing growth during the past five years. He has a very bright team, but surprisingly, much of the institution's growth has come from areas other than those suggested by its strategic planning exercises. In fact, growth has centered on programs conceived and implemented in a relatively short time as a direct result of intense interaction and dialog with outside experts (customers and donors) who have pragmatically and psychologically been brought inside the organization. Based on their informed comments and competencies as well as on other corporate observations, knowledge has been created within the organization that has contributed to a new level of value satisfaction as well as new programming.

Planning has not been the enemy here. How do you plan in an unsure environment? Heightened competition and rapid communication have already begun to make obsolete many traditional paths to competitive strategy. However, creating a stakeholder-centric focus within your organization can become critical if you want to change how you permanently operate and, if you also want to dramatically affect the ways current and prospective customers, donors, and volunteers experience you. Although there are many immediate actions an agency can take to become competitive, if being consumed with stakeholder behavior is not one of them, change efforts in the long run will matter very little. Without systematic and real change, as opposed to the narrow change that typically comes with an almost exclusive desire for short-term wins, and a willingness to disturb habitual ways of responding to customers and supporters, no real assimilation of new data, vision, and capabilities can take place.

Lasting causal innovation can take place only if there are fundamental changes in how an institution creates knowledge, where idea generation occurs, how all functional areas participate, and, ultimately, what type of culture exists within the agency. Because so many third-sector institutions are streamlining their processes, shrinking costs, and saving time in ways that are alternately replicated by everyone else, most nonprofit agencies compete by trying to differentiate themselves from one another. The only real, sustainable differentiation comes when an institution changes how it does business in relationship to its knowledge creation and value provision for its supportive constituency. The creation of new value for the stakeholder is ultimately tied to the creation of new knowledge in the guise of value innovation. When stakeholders are allowed to help in the creation of value for themselves and for the organizations they support, a stakeholder relationship develops, causal innovation takes place, and the organization's systems, social structure, and infrastructure are affected positively. In addition, the cause differentiates itself by bundling outside competencies with those inside, creating new knowledge and expanding the borders of the cause. In this way it succeeds in building a third-sector cause that prospers in pursuit of its goals.

Index